Growing Koa: A Hawaiian Legacy Tree

Kim M. Wilkinson and Craig R. Elevitch

PAR

Growing Koa: A Hawaiian Legacy Tree

Published by:
Permanent Agriculture Resources (PAR)
P.O. Box 428
Holualoa, HI 96725 USA
E-mail: par@agroforestry.net
Web: http://www.agroforestry.net

First Edition January 2003

ISBN 0-9702544-2-3

Library of Congress Control Number: 2002115085

Printed in Korea by USAsia Press
This book is printed on acid-free paper

Recommended citation:

Wilkinson, K.M. and C.R. Elevitch. 2003. Growing Koa: A Hawaiian Legacy Tree. Permanent Agriculture Resources, Holualoa, Hawai'i, USA. Web site: http://www.agroforestry.net

Cover photo: Koa forest regenerates on former pasture at Honokohau, Hawai'i

Contents

Dedicated to the
Wao Lipo

The *wao lipo* is that forested region where the tallest trees grow and the deepest shadows fall. *Wao lipo*, where mists waft, silently drenching the branches. *Wao lipo*, where the sunlight falls in shafts, creating dapples of dark and bright. *Wao lipo*, where the otherworldly and the worldly mingle, even court each other. *Wao lipo,* where the *koa* is the tallest of the tall, casting the deepest shadows of them all.

The shadow that *koa* casts crosses the deepest seas, in effect from the *wao lipo* to the *kai lipo*. *Kai lipo* the deepest, darkest sea. It is perhaps in its incarnation as a racing canoe that the *koa* has touched the most of us. The racing canoe is the current generation of a lineage that reaches into the voyaging past and which includes the pelagic fishing fleets that plied island waters into the twentieth century. Whether or not we have personally paddled the waters of the Kaiwi Channel between the islands of Molokaʻi and Oʻahu, we may have relatives or friends who have, we may have seen the news announcements or reports of the race, we may have seen the television coverage of it. "It" began in the *wao lipo*, distant generations ago when a canoe maker first selected *koa*, as his tree of choice.

Canoe makers learned myriad forest lore that assured their selections would be appropriate for their needs. They were joined in the forests by bird hunters coming for protein as well as plumage and woodsmen who gathered other timber and fiber products and herbalists who came for medicinal materials. In traditional times those who entered the *wao lipo* came according to protocols which assured an orderly relationship between the patron deities of the forest, of canoe making, bird hunting, forestry, and herbology and the men who pursued those vocations.

As the human population grew the lowland forests retreated. The *wao kanaka*, the region where men dwell and work, expanded. The relationship between the old gods and the men newly arrived to the shores of Hawaiʻi strained to the point that even those descended from the ancient voyagers no longer maintained the protocols which had ordered and maintained the balance between the men and the forests.

The forests, even the deepest, continue to retreat before the woodsmen's saws, the ranchers' bulldozers, and the developers' subdivisions. The forests, even the deepest, continue to change as native species diminish and alien species become established and dominate them. The forests, especially the deepest, continue to inspire those among us who have ventured into them.

They remain a living legacy whether we have known the deepest shade or not. It is the forests which fetch the rains and keep their moisture close to us. It is the forests that make right again the air for us to breathe. It is the forests which yield so many things we need and even more that we want to make our lives full.

It is a matter of perspective, the choices that we make and the manner in which we pursue them. This book is about the growing of *koa*, and so much more. As a manual, it teaches us well about why and how to prepare the land for planting, why and how to plant, and why and how to maintain the planted areas. This book also offers us a glimpse into the lives of people who have dedicated thoughtfulness and energy and the resources of land and labor to the working of *koa*, whether as a forester or a botanist, a woodworker or a landowner, a naturalist or a navigator.

This book may be a guide back to the *wao lipo*. The *koa* is certainly not the only member of the complex ecosystem that the ancients called the *wao lipo*, but it is the one that grows the tallest and casts the deepest shade.

Thank you.

Hannah Kihalani Springer
Ka'ūpūlehu, North Kona

Acknowledgments

Working with koa and writing this book has been humbling as well as uplifting. There are many, many people whose understanding could fill volumes, who taught us, and influenced us in authoring this book.

We are deeply grateful to Muriel and Kent Lighter, whose generous grant made the publication of this book possible. In addition to printing costs, their grant supported the donation of 250 copies to libraries, schools and educational organizations throughout Hawai'i. We are moved by their confidence and support.

The grant was administered with aplomb and aloha by the Big Island Resource Conservation & Development Council, Inc. Over the decades they have also organized conferences and sessions focused on koa, whose proceedings are of immense value.

A special thanks to Hannah Springer and Mike Tomich. Hannah gifted the book with a deeply moving and inspiring dedication.

We have been so fortunate to receive the helping hands of reviewers with enormous practical experience: Rogerene (Kali) Montero Arce, Extension Agent, UH-Manoa Department of Tropical Plant and Soil Sciences; Jill Wagner, Tropical Reforestation & Ecosystems Education (TREE) Center; J.B. Friday, Extension Forester, CTAHR-UH Manoa; Ron Peyton, District Conservationist (retired), Natural Resources Conservation Service (NRCS); Heidi Bornhorst, Director, Honolulu Botanical Gardens; Marty Fernandes, Horticulturist, Na Aina Kai Botanical Gardens; and Aileen Yeh of the Hawaii Agriculture Research Center (HARC). Reviewers made detailed comments on the text, checked facts, and made themselves available for all manner of questions. Of course, the authors are fully responsible for any errors that may remain!

Thanks to Nick Dudley for nearly a decade of generous counseling and support on tree improvement and seed selection for koa and other species. J.B. Friday has elevated and encouraged better farm forestry and forestry throughout Hawai'i. He provided a number of hard-to-find references that enriched the book, and also provided some lucid editing and guidance. Kelly Greenwell has freely shared his knowledge of reforestation with us for the past decade and hosted us alone and in groups for numerous tours of his project, and taught us a great deal about koa forest regeneration. Bart Potter dedicated many hours of time and thoughtfulness to this book and made available his extensive collection of photographs and experiences. Brian Bushe diagnosed and wrote the text covering a large number of koa pests and diseases shown in this book, which was especially challenging given that he was working only with photographs. Karl Dalla Rosa has encouraged us in the planning process and in participation with the Forest Stewardship Program. Roger Imoto helped us early on in our work with koa reforestation.

We deeply appreciate those who generously shared their experiences for Chapter 9, "Perspectives" on page 65: Patrick Baker, Heidi Bornhorst, Nick Dudley, J. B. Friday, Kelly Greenwell, Mel Johansen, Kanoa Kimball, Mark Kimball, Candace Lutzow-Felling, Rob Pacheco, Benton Keali'i Pang, Bart Potter, Ernest Pung, Sally Rice, Paul Scowcroft, Peter Simmons, Roger Skolmen, and Nainoa Thompson.

There are a number of brave and dedicated people who have been planting koa and other native trees, and we are grateful to have been able to share in the process with Mark, K.B., and Kanoa Kimball, Jeff and Carol Seel, Nancy Jones, Desmond Twigg-Smith, Clinton Strong, Charles Anderson, Muriel and Kent Lighter, Ellen Mehos, Sally Rice,

David Rietow, John Florek, James Coffey, Mark Smith, Christian Twigg-Smith, Bill Cowern, and many others.

Thanks to the staff of the former Nitrogen Fixing Tree Association in Waimanalo who fueled our interest in the restoration abilities of trees such as koa. They include Bill Macklin, Charles Sorenson, Nancy Glover, James Brewbaker, Erin Moore, James Roshetko, Mark Powell, and Eric Brennan. We are thankful to Harold Keyser, Paul Singleton and Padma Somasegaran of the NifTAL Project (Nitrogen Fixation by Tropical Agricultural Legumes) of the University of Hawai'i, Paia, Hawai'i, for their research and dedication to biological nitrogen fixation and rhizobia inoculants. We are also very grateful to Mitiku Habte of the University of Hawai'i, Department of Agronomy and Soil Science for sharing his extensive knowledge of mycorrhizal fungi. Tom Landis, the nursery specialist at the USDA Forest Service, assisted and encouraged us in the fledgling stages of growing trees for forestry. We have also been inspired by the productivity of the State Tree Nursery over the years, and continually received friendly support from Jeanine Lum, Charles Labrador, and Jay Hatayama.

A special thanks to Norman Allen. Norman, Curtis Yamauchi, Bill Rosehill, and the Keoua-Honaunau Canoe Club shared photos and information about the making of the Ka'ahumanu koa canoe. Jaroslav "Jay" Ludvick shared fascinating stories of his career in the koa forests. Thanks to naturalists Jon Young, Doniga Murdoch, and all the staff and volunteers of the Wilderness Awareness School who helped open our eyes to even more of the forest.

People who contributed photographs greatly enriched this book, including Monte Costa, Jack Jeffrey, David Gomes, Jay Hatayama, Marion Yasuda, John DeMello, Bart Potter, Annie Rogers, David Higa, Doug Mastaler, Bill Rosehill, Pat Felling, Coleen Carroll, Brent Sipes, Lou Lambert, and Carl Waldbauer. A number of organizations have been especially helpful to us in the past and/or with the production of this book, and we extend a special aloha to the The Tropical Reforestation and Ecosystem Recovery Center, Hawai'i Forest Industry Association, the Polynesian Voyaging Society, and the Kona Pacific School.

Our communication coach and dear friend Kerry King was available at all hours and for all aspects of this book, both personal and professional. His support added immeasurably to the process of realizing our vision.

Our parents and siblings have given us tremendous support in following our paths. We send thanks and love to Edward, Kathleen, Amy and Heather Wilkinson, to Frank, JoAnn, and Jill Elevitch, and to Kim's aunt Lanie Murphy and late grandmother Joan Murphy. It is our families who laid the foundation for our lives.

We honor and thank all people who care about koa, those we have met in the course of our work so far and those we look forward to meeting in the future. You inspire us. Awareness of the importance of protecting and perpetuating koa and its ecosystems is on the rise, thanks to the focus and dedication of many people like you.

Mahalo nui loa.

Kim M. Wilkinson and Craig R. Elevitch
Hōlualoa, North Kona

Chapter 1: Introduction

The Hawaiian Islands rose volcanically from the ocean to become one of the most remote land masses on earth. They were originally bare, devoid of plant life. Over eons, seeds and spores were brought in by wind, waves, and far traveling birds, and a few managed to take root on the new land. One of these, carried perhaps by a lone storm-blown bird over a million years ago, evolved into a tree unique in all the world: the Hawaiian koa.

Koa became the largest of the native Hawaiian trees, dominating the canopy of many Hawaiian forests on the main islands of the archipelago. It grew from the lowland forests to the upland mountains. One of only a handful of native trees capable of fixing nitrogen, koa enriches the soil around it, providing essential fertility to the plants nearby by dropping its nitrogen-rich leaf litter. The huge trees themselves provide life-giving niches for other plant life, including ferns, vines, fungi, lichens, and epiphytes.

Koa seeds fed some birds and insects directly, and thousands of other species of birds, snails, spiders and insects made their homes in koa, foraged for food off its bark, twigs, or leaves, and lived their lives in the koa trees. While many of these birds and insects are now extinct, those that remain still depend on koa and koa forests for habitat. Over fifty species of insects found nowhere else on earth evolved specifically for koa. The Kamehameha Butterfly, the native Blackburn's Butterfly, and the Koa bug favor koa. The abundance and distribution of most endangered forest birds including Hawaiian honeycreepers, the 'akiapola'au, and the 'akepa are strongly linked to koa. Koa trees also affect the climate, building the water holding capacity of soils, accumulating condensation and fog drip, and cooling the air.

Because of its essential ecosystem functions, with so many other living things supported

Life found its way to the remote Hawaiian Islands and evolved into unique forms not found anywhere else on earth

directly or indirectly, koa is a key species in the ecology of the Hawaiian forests.

When people first arrived in the islands, koa became one of the most important trees to human culture and economy as well. Koa is recognized as the Monarch of Hawaiian forests. It is also one of the world's most valuable hardwoods. What is meant by the proverb *E ola koa*, "Live like a koa tree" can be pondered endlessly.

While as a species koa is not at risk of becoming endangered or threatened, the once extensive koa forests are severely diminished. Only about 10% of the original koa forests are left. Many of the species of plants and animals associated with koa have gone extinct, and many of those that remain are endangered. In addition, the beautiful and unique koa wood

'Ākiapola'au (photo: Jack Jeffrey)

so fundamental to Hawaiian culture was named as a "vanishing timber" by the National Academy of Sciences in 1979 (Rachie et al 1979).

When the Native Hawaiian Culture and Arts Program set out to build a voyaging canoe of traditional materials in 1990's, they searched the forests and could not find a single koa tree sizable enough to make even one of the hulls of the Hawai'iloa (see perspective of Nainoa Thompson on page 65). Protecting, planting, and regenerating koa has become a concern of all people who care about Hawai'i.

Koa and Humans

Early Hawaiians created a rich and sophisti-cated culture as they settled Hawai'i. In a land lacking in most of the resources such as metals and clays that enrich other material cultures, the presence of enormous koa trees with their strong, beautiful wood was a tremendous boon. Koa was and is used to build the Hawaiian canoe, considered by many to be the most seaworthy and versatile rough-water craft ever developed by any culture (Holmes 1981). These canoes ranged in size from smaller fishing, racing, and war craft to massive voyaging vessels over 100 feet (30 m) long. The flotillas of canoes on the ocean were sometimes referred to as "the koa grove at

sea" (Pukui 1983). A koa racing canoe is still the pride of any Canoe Club. The koa canoe is a technological achievement by any standards, and uniquely Hawaiian as the only voyaging craft in all Polynesia to employ a solid, one-piece hull (Holmes 1981).

Koa wood was also used to make surfboards (some up to 18 ft (5.5 m) long), paddles, spear handles, bowls, non-food calabashes, and occasionally used as frames for grass huts. Early Hawaiians, however, did not use wood furniture, homes, flooring or wall paneling.

Koa trees had deep spiritual significance in the Hawaiian culture. The upland forests were largely protected by strict *kapu* systems, and only highly trained specialists (*kahuna*) were permitted to enter them (see perspective of Benton Keali'i Pang on page 67). Commen-surate naturalists, early Hawaiians were sensitive to the importance of upland koa forests for watershed and a healthy island ecology. The proverb *Hahai no ka ua i ka ulula'au* ("Rains always follow the forest") is an example of this understanding (Pukui 1983).

Launch of the Ka'ahumanu, a koa racing canoe (photo: Bill Rosehill, courtesy Keoua-Honaunau Canoe Club)

There is debate as to how much upland koa forest was affected by early Hawaiians. Lowlands had been burned, altered, and deforested for agriculture and settlements (Cuddihy and Stone 1990). But it is certain that large koa abounded in the forests at the arrival of Captain Cook; in 1779 his lieutenant Charles Clerke wrote of the forest above Kealakekua: "Some of our explorers…measured a tree of 19 feet in its girth and rising very proportionally in its bulk to a great height, nor did this far, if at all, exceed in stateliness many of its neighbors…" (Holmes 1981, quoting Beaglehole 1976). Botanist Archibald Menzies reported fourteen years later, "I measured two of them…one of which was 17 feet and the other about 18 feet in circumference with straight trunks 40 or 50 feet high, and strong, bold spreading branches" (Jenkins 1983, quoting Menzies 1920).

The introduction of Western ways led to the spread of Western wood uses, and also to Western concepts of land ownership and resource exploitation.

What Happened to the Koa Forests?

A complex and interlocking series of human-induced changes altered the face of Hawai'i's forests, including land clearing, livestock, logging, climate change, fire, and introduced pests and diseases.

Foremost among these was the introduction of cattle and other livestock. Livestock had, and still have, an enormous detrimental impact on Hawaiian forests. Early Hawaiians had introduced small pigs to the islands, which later interbred with larger European pigs. Captain George Vancouver introduced the first cattle to Hawai'i as a gift to King Kamehameha in 1793. Goats, sheep, deer, and other large animals followed. In an environment without native land mammals excepting a small bat, Hawaiian plants evolved defenseless against grazing or browsing animals, without the thorns, repellent tastes, toxins, spines, or unappetizing smells that protect vegetation in other parts of the world (with a few notable thorny exceptions that might have protected some plants from the now extinct three feet tall geese). Most native plants, especially koa

Right: **An old giant, now protected in a conservation area (pictured: Mel Johansen)**

seedlings, are delicious to grazing and browsing animals.

Koa seedlings, bark, and root systems are attractive forage for livestock, actively sought out and relished by many animals. While the older trees died, any tender young seedlings trying take their place would be quickly devoured. Hundreds of thousands of livestock proliferated and ran wild, reaching even inaccessible slopes previously impenetrable to humans (Culliney 1988). As the forests died back under the onslaught, the climate began to change, growing hotter and dryer, which created even more open vegetation and even easier access for voracious grazing animals while increasing the risks of fires. There are some areas where large koa trees died without any logging taking place, as a result of climate change and tromping by animals.

Cattle have played a major role in the destruction of koa forests

A shift in thinking had also taken place. The *kapu* (traditional sacred law) system had been officially dissolved before the arrival of missionaries by King Kamehameha II (Lihiliho) and his stepmother Ka'ahumanu at the end of the year 1819. Having witnessed Western visitors unwittingly breaking time-honored traditions seemingly without conse-quence, the strict regulations were viewed as unfounded and restricting. Even today, some descriptions of the *kapu* system take a rather ridiculing tone when pointing out some of the socially oppressive laws. However, it may

have been a case of throwing the baby out with the bath water; while some of the *kapu* regulations were designed to enforce social hierarchies, others were based on millennia of resource management and intimacy with nature. With the accompanying devaluation (some might say "demonization" later encouraged by missionaries) of traditional *kahuna* and craft masters, the indigenous protective system of the upland forests was discarded. At the same time, the traditional wisdom and holistic understanding of ecology that had been passed down orally from generation to generation of skilled naturalists over a thousand years was put down. It was replaced by a more simplistic, exploitative and shortsighted view backed by increasing numbers of newcomers.

Koa logging became an established industry in the 1830's. As the new wave of immigrants expanded, homes and churches constructed in this period are notable for their lavish use koa wood. Vast expanses of koa flooring and wall paneling, enormous pieces of solid koa furniture, and koa used as house frames can be a shock to the modern eye accustomed to today's scarcity and high price of koa wood.

The Mahele of the late 1840's was another blow, allowing ownership rights of land to "commoners" (including foreigners) while defacto depriving most Hawaiians of theirs. It was during this time that many koa forests were razed for their lumber. Systematic defor-estation and land clearing began in earnest, and by the 1850's more sawmills had opened and massive clearcutting of koa was underway. In one area above Waimea on the Big Island, the Hawaiians seeing the massive stacks of koa lumber piled near Hanaipoe, gave the area the name Paliho'oukapapa, which means "cliffs of piled lumber" (Culliney 1988).

The Mahele also led to the dividing of newly declared land parcels and the building of inroads and trails, which further fragmented the forests. Other activities such as the uncon-trolled harvest of hapu'u ferns (*Cibotium* sp.) for cheap packing material and mattress stuffing further opened the understory of some forests and gave access to encroaching livestock and accompanying foreign insects, diseases, and plant seeds (Culliney 1988).

It did not take long. For example, the following description written by George Washington Bates describes an area south of Waimea, Hawai'i less than 150 years ago: "...dense forest of gigantic koa, covered with delicate creepers. There were noble specimens of the tree fern..." (Skolmen 1986, quoting Bates 1854) This area is now very open, dry grassland with only about twenty inches (510 mm) of rain a year.

As another example, a description made by naturalist John Ledyard in 1779 regarding a site at 4,000 feet (1,220 m) elevation above Kealekekua: "A number of fine birds of the liveliest and most variegated plumage that any of us ever met with...The woods here are thick and luxuriant, the largest trees being nearly thirty feet in girth, and these with the shrubbery underneath, and the whole inter-sected with vines, render it very umbrageous" (Walker 1986, quoting MacCaughey 1918). This same site was described by botanist E.F. Rock in 1913: "Above Kealakekua, South Kona, of the once beautiful koa forest, 90 percent of the trees are now dead, and the remaining 10 percent in a dying condition. Their huge trunks and limbs now cover the ground so thickly that it is difficult to ride through the forest, if such it can be called...It is sad, however, to see these gigantic trees succumb to the ravages of cattle and insects" (Whitesell 1990, quoting Rock 1913).

Koa forests were also injured by some misguided prejudices of past practices that devalued native trees as inferior to introduc-tions, leading not only to native forest destruction in some areas with the purpose of planting exotic trees, but also the promotion of new and potentially invasive introductions instead of native and Polynesian trees.

Today, the shortsightedness of past resource use is recognized, and many of Hawai'i's people are dedicated to finding ways to conserve, plant and regenerate koa and other native species, while protecting Hawai'i's priceless ecological and cultural heritage.

Koa Wood Today

The beauty of koa wood was recognized by the Hawaiians and later by European explorers, who noted the magnificent wood on the Hawaiian canoes. But the first missionary settlers utilized koa more out of necessity for items to make their own homes more comfortable. Furniture soon became a status symbol for new immigrants as well as Hawaiians of high standing. As Hawaiian *ali'i* (royalty) traveled the world, they brought back with them a taste for European style furniture and homes. Woodworkers and cabinetmakers from Europe, China, and Japan opened shop in Hawai'i.

Koa was sold in the mid-1800's for about 4¢ per board foot. Even in the early 1980's, koa was priced as low as 30¢ a board foot—and was sometimes sold by the truckload (Ludvick, p. comm). There are many people in Hawai'i who remember koa wood used not only for fine woodworking but as firewood and fence posts.

However, increasing scarcity, a deeper recog-nition for the uniqueness of the tree and its wood, and renewed and growing appreciation for native Hawaiian culture has finally allowed koa wood to be valued more appro-priately. Koa wood is now priced from about $8 up to over $35 per board foot, depending on the grade. This places it among the most expensive woods in the world. Most high-value koa wood is still essentially 'mined,' usually as salvage from dead or dying trees in pasture land. Koa wood remains scarce largely because in past decades koa forests have not regenerated at a healthy rate, either naturally or with human help.

However, the economic value is fueling greater attention to the species and its forest ecosystems from all sectors. Sustainable forest management, reforestation and conservation efforts are encouraged by koa's high value, and it may turn out one day that koa is a

Ukulele by David Gomes (photo: David Gomes)

Planting and Perpetuating Koa

Current thinking is to prevent further losses and extinctions of endangered native Hawaiian plants and animals by protecting large areas of forests, ideally entire ecosystems. It is not enough to set these areas aside; they must be actively managed to control invasive plants and animals so the native species can be regenerated.

species where conservation and sustainable economic needs can find a happy marriage.

Today, objects made from koa are valued as the unique treasures they are. Fine furniture, musical instruments, turnery, carvings, crafts, picture frames, and even pens made of koa wood are cherished by their owners.

Today, koa is prized, with high emphasis on responsible management. *Below:* Koa chest by Marian Yasuda (photo: John DeMello)

Koa reforestation, Hakalau Wildlife Refuge

Even conservation areas have been altered and degraded by livestock and by other human activity. In these cases, koa is sometimes planted to modify and enrich harsh conditions, eventually making areas more hospitable for replanting less hardy native plants and creating wildlife corridors.

Koa is a key ecological species, a cornerstone of many Hawaiian ecosystems. Planting koa alone will not bring back the native forest. However, it is a place to start, and many people with a love of plants and Hawai'i want to grow koa in landscapes, school grounds, rural areas, or small-scale reforestation projects on private land.

Planting koa can bring a deeper understanding of this tree that is central to Hawai'i's ecology, culture, and economy. Planting koa also restores this tree to environments where it once lived, and can live again.

Chapter 2: About the Koa Tree

Koa's range within the Hawaiian Islands was once vast, from the lowland forests up to the mountains, in dry and moist forests, from 300 feet up to 7,000 feet (90 to 2,134 m), occasionally as low as 80 feet (24 m) and, rarely, as high as 8,000 feet (2,440 m). Koa is intolerant of salt, which is why it does not grow on the coast; and also sensitive to frost, which is why it does not thrive in Hawai'i's subarctic regions. It is found on all six major Hawaiian Islands: Hawai'i, Moloka'i, Maui, Lana'i, O'ahu, and Kaua'i (Whitesell 1990).

Today, the largest and most thriving koa are found at elevations between 3,000 and 6,000 feet (915 and 1,830 m). At elevations below 2,000 feet (610 m), pests, diseases, grazing animals, and other factors threaten the health of koa trees. However, koa can be planted at these lower elevations, and in fact doing so may be one of the ways to foster a future seed source adapted to areas that once were, and could again be, koa forest.

Variability

Koa trees are variable in almost every way imaginable. From one population to another, and even from one individual to another, the differences are dramatic. Some koa trees are small, shrubby and multi-branched; some are tall and straight. On some koa, the "leaves" (technically flattened leaf stems called phyllodes) are wide and short; others are narrow and long. Some koa produce very small seeds (up to 7,500 seeds per pound), and some produce much larger seeds (less than 2,500 per pound).

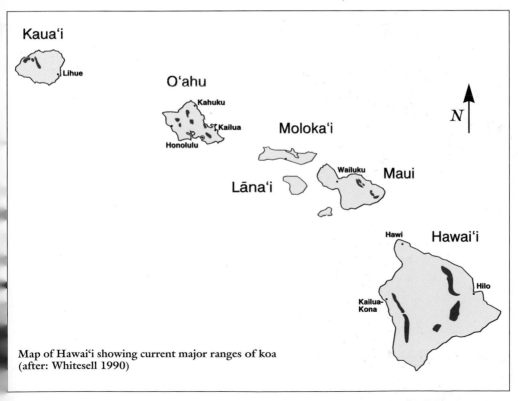

Map of Hawai'i showing current major ranges of koa
(after: Whitesell 1990)

KOA DESCRIPTION AND BOTANY

Species name: *Acacia koa*
Family: Fabaceae (legume family)
Subfamily: Mimosoideae
Genus: *Acacia*
Subgenus: *Heterophyllum*
General: Large, evergreen broadleaf tree
Form: From tall and straight to spreading and low
Bark: Light gray, smooth when young, thick and rough on older trees
Roots: Extensive shallow, spreading roots; can sucker
Flowers: Pale yellow, clustered into "puff balls" averaging 0.33 inches (8.5 mm) in diameter.

Leaves: Young seedlings have bipinnate compound true leaves with 12–24 pairs of leaflets. Mature koa have no true leaves, but only phyllodes (flattened leaf stems), sickle-shaped.
Pods: About 6–8 inches (15–20 cm) long, containing 6–12 seeds. Can seed any time of year.
Traditional wood uses: Canoes, surfboards, house frames, non-food calabashes, spear handles.
Current wood uses: Canoes, furniture, cabinetry, musical instruments, carving, turnery, veneers.

Other uses/significance: Tannin derived from koa bark was used to make a red dye for *kapa* cloth (a fabric made from the bark of wauke, *Broussonetia papyrifera*). Koa leaves and ashes were used medicinally. Koa also had ceremonial significance.
Significance: The word koa also means "brave, bold, and fearless," and "warrior or hero." A small koa was sometimes added to the altar of the goddess of the hula, Laka, "to make the dancer fearless" (Pukui and Elbert 1986).

Top Left: Flowering branch; *Top Center:* Seed pods; *Top Right:* Seeds; *Middle Row Left:* True leaves; *Middle Row Center*: The transition to "mature leaves," technically called phyllodes; *Middle Row Right*: Mature tree; *Lower Left:* Typical surface roots (trampled by foot traffic); *Lower Center:* Young smooth bark; *Lower Right:* Rough mature bark.

Early Hawaiians developed a complex classification system for koa, identifying factors including tree shape, form, size, grain, branching patterns, and much more. A few examples of the terminology used in identifying koa for canoes include (after Holmes 1981):

koa hiʻu waʻa: growing straight up before branching

koa huhui: growing straight up, with a cluster of branches at the top

koa koʻamoku: large and rounded but not long; a canoe made from this type will have the same width from stern to prow

koa kolo: leaning or sprawling, but still fit for use

koa lau nui: a large leafed variety

koa noʻu: straight, thick, unblemished, not very tall; suitable for a wide, short canoe

koa poepoe: of good size but short and thick

koa laʻau maiʻa: "banana-colored;" lightweight wood used for paddles, rarely used for canoes

koa ʻiʻo ʻōhiʻa: extremely dense, heavy weight wood so hard to work it was avoided for canoes

koa lau kani: strong; considered male

Koa's form and size is highly variable. *Left:* A straight tree with a single, main stem; *Right:* A tree with numerous co-dominant branches

Koa wood characteristics are amazingly variable. Koa wood can range from a blonde, low-density wood to very dark, heavy, and deeply figured. Cabinetmakers recognize over a dozen types of koa wood, including yellow koa, red koa, and curly or "fiddle back" koa (Whitesell 1990). Some of these wood characteristics are thought to be genetic; others might be more closely related to the conditions in which the tree was grown.

Left: **Master canoe builder Jacques Wong and son Jean-Pierre construct the koa racing canoe-Kaʻahumanu.** *Right:* **Blessing of the Kaʻahumanu by Lanakila Brandt (photos: Bill Rosehill, courtesy Keoua-Honaunau Canoe Club)**

Koa wood quality and color can vary dramatically from tree to tree. *Above Left:* Difference in coloration with strong curl (Round Top, Oʻahu); *Above Center:* Very intense curl and dark color banding (Round Top, Oʻahu); *Above Right:* Light colored and very curly tree (Kona, Hawaiʻi)

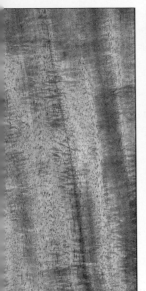

Left: Plain with light flame (Kalihi, Oʻahu); *Left center:* No curl (Kona, Hawaiʻi); *Right center:* Extraordinarily dark but rather plain (Kona, Hawaiʻi); *Right:* Blister figure—what appears as blister on the flat cut will show up as a curl on the quarter cut (Kona, Hawaiʻi) (All above wood images courtesy C. Barton Potter Co.)

Look-a-likes: There are a number of trees that are often confused with koa. *Left:* Koaiʻa is a wonderful native Hawaiian tree distinguished from koa in several ways, including smaller stature and phyllodes; *Center:* Formosan koa (*Acacia confusa*) has much smaller spiky leaves and bright yellow flowers, and is a frequent (and potentially invasive) ornamental in dry areas; *Right:* Haole koa (*Leucaena leucocephala*) has leaves similar to those of young koa, however this is an invasive species in many lowland areas

Koa's Vital Role in Forest Fertility: Nitrogen Fixation

People who grow plants know that nitrogen is a nutrient necessary for any plant to be green, healthy, and growing. Farmers and gardeners apply manures and other nitrogen fertilizers to their crops. But in the forest, plants are verdant and healthy. Huge trees thrive, and understory plants are green and lush. Where are they getting their nitrogen fertility?

Koa and other nitrogen fixing plants have the ability, through a symbiotic association with certain soil bacteria, to take nitrogen out of the air and use it for growth. Koa is one of only five native Hawaiian trees that provide nitrogen fertility to the ecosystem.

Nature has an immense reserve of nitrogen everywhere plants grow—in the air. Air consists of approximately 80% nitrogen gas (N_2), representing thousands of pounds of nitrogen above every acre of land. However, N_2 is a stable gas, normally unavailable to plants. Nitrogen fixation is a process by which certain soil bacteria on the roots of nitrogen fixing plants "fix" or gather nitrogen from the air, and allow their tree hosts to incorporate it into their leaves and tissues. The tree provides energy to feed the bacteria and fuel the nitrogen fixation process. In return, the tree receives nitrogen for growth

The atmospheric nitrogen is then incorporated into the tree's leaves and tissues. When the tree drops its leaves or dies back, that nitrogen goes into the ecosystem to be utilized as fertilizer by other plants in the forest.

This process of accumulating atmospheric nitrogen in plants and recycling it through organic matter is a major source of nitrogen fertility in tropical ecosystems. Land rehabilitation practices employ this natural fertility process by using nitrogen fixing trees such as koa to restore ecosystem function and return fertility to the land.

Because it enriches Hawai'i's otherwise nitrogen-poor volcanic soils and nourishes the plants around it, koa is a key species of many Hawaiian forest ecosystems.

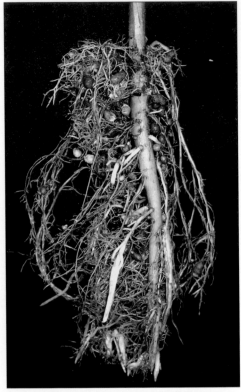

Root system of a koa seedling showing nodules where nitrogen fixation takes place.

Other Native Hawaiian Nitrogen Fixing Trees

Koa is one of only five native Hawaiian nitrogen fixing trees. The other four are: koai'a (*Acacia koaia*), wiliwili (*Erythrina sandwicensis*), 'ohai (*Sesbania tomentosa*) and mamane (*Sophora chrysophylla*). With the exception of wiliwili, which is found on some other Pacific Islands, all of these trees are endemic to Hawai'i, meaning they are found nowhere else in the world.

Environmental Preferences and Tolerances

Koa can grow in areas that receive as little as 25 inches (640 mm) of rain a year. Fastest growth is thought to be achieved in areas that receive 75–200 inches (1,900–5,000 mm) of rain a year. In drier conditions, growth will be slower and form may be poorer; however, drier conditions are thought to possibly favor more beautiful wood.

Koa trees have shallow root systems, and can grow well as long soil is at least three feet deep (1 m) and moderately well-drained. On shallow soils over pahoehoe lava, koa seedlings may be blown over by wind after several years of growth. Koa are thought to perform better on a'a lava than on pahoehoe lava (Ares and Fownes 1999).

Koa trees do not tolerate salt, constant water-logging (as in wet rainforest conditions), or shade. In some areas, diseases and pests can thwart the long-term growth and survival of planted koa trees. *Fusarium* root rot and black twig borers are some of the most common problems in lower elevation areas. It is believed that planting from local seed sources results in trees that are better adapted to local site conditions. Even so, growing koa in low elevation areas where it once lived is still considered experimental.

How Big Do Koa Grow?

A koa tree can become enormous, exceeding 100 feet (30 m) in height and 6 feet (1.8 m) in diameter, with a canopy spread of 40–80 feet (12–24 m). More commonly, though, they are much smaller; usually less than half that size at maturity. Trees from certain areas of the islands of Hawai'i and Kaua'i tend to be the straightest and tallest; those from other islands usually are much smaller and shrubbier (Little and Skolmen 1989). Seed source selection can help growers obtain trees with the most desirable characteristics for their needs. Landscapers, for example, might prefer smaller-maturing trees, while foresters prefer larger koa.

Koa seedlings are moderately fast growing. The growth rate depends on the site conditions, management, and the quality of the seedling itself. After one year of growth, seedling size can range from 2–14 feet (0.6–4.3 m) tall, with 6 feet (1.8 m) being about average. After five years on a good site, trees may be 20–30 feet (6–9 m) tall.

Some Ways People Plant Koa

School/educational projects: As a relatively easy-to-propagate and fast-growing native tree with deep importance to Hawaiian culture and ecology, growing koa can be a wonderful way for children to connect to the *ʻaina.*

Landscaping: Except for coastal areas or poorly drained soils, koa can grow as specimen trees in landscapes. Koa casts a dappled shade that allows for understory planting. It must be given sufficient space to grow, as the shallow root systems are aggressive and can cause problems to utility lines or by competing with other plants. It most appropriate for larger-scale landscapes,

although select seed sources might yield smaller-maturing trees. In lowland areas, some koa might succumb to disease after about a decade of growth.

Farm forestry and small-scale reforestation: Anyone with an extra quarter acre (0.1 hectare) or more should consider what native trees they can foster. Koa is an attractive choice to plant for farm foresters and small-scale reforestation projects. As a nitrogen-fixing species, koa is also planted for land restoration or in areas otherwise unsuitable for agriculture. Many such projects are not focused on economic returns, but instead plant koa as a way to enjoy meaningful family activity, beautiful trees, and the hope of leaving a legacy for future generations.

Conservation and large-scale reforestation: Regenerating koa is key to restoring ecosystem function and eventually wildlife habitat in Hawaiian forests. Some of these projects also hope to regenerate the supply of "canoe koa" for the future, serving economic, cultural and conservation goals.

Get Ready to Plant!

Koa trees are long-term elements in any landscape. The first step in planting koa is planning to plant.

Chapter 3: Planning

Planning is essential, even if just a few trees are to be planted. Koa trees are long term elements on the land. Successful establishment involves planning and action over several years—a "plant it and forget it" strategy will most likely be unsuccessful. In addition, koa trees grow large and have a big impact on sun, views and visibility. Good planning and design precludes or minimizes any potential problems, while maximizing the benefits of the trees.

Who is the Planner?

The person ultimately responsible for carrying out and maintaining the planting project over time must be intimately involved in the planning process. This is usually the landholder. For a larger project, the landholder may engage the services of a forestry planner, resource consultant, soil and water conservation agent, cultural advisor, landscaper, and others. However, only the landholder can consider and balance all the elements and develop a plan that will successfully be implemented over time. Therefore, it is best that the landholder is the lead planner.

Strategic vs. Master Planning

Some growers may feel skeptical about the concept of developing a plan; many picture a paper version of a fixed end goal, a "blueprint" type of planning. The purpose of planning a tree planting is not to create a blueprint, but rather to create a flexible framework for development. As General Eisenhower once said: "Plans are useless, but planning is essential." This statement can be read to mean that "A Master Plan as a blueprint on paper is useless, but Strategic Planning, the process of planning, is essential" (Holmgren 1994).

The landholder is in charge of carrying out their vision (pictured: Nancy Jones)

Master planning may work for a solid, permanent structure made of static materials, but when that kind of planning is applied to a living, growing system, its value is limited.

In contrast, while Strategic Planning involves targeting desired future results, it recognizes that complex systems cannot be completely predicted or controlled. Strategic planning is an ongoing process of development. It is written and/or sketched out with the target and direction in mind, taking into account the needs, goals, and vision for the future. The plan evolves over time and can be adapted to changing situations, such as changing priorities, new information, shifting weather conditions, resource availability, and so forth.

Strategic planning allows for the unpredictability of nature (pictured: enrichment planting of koa with 'ōhi'a)

- How far apart are the thriving, mature koa trees? How much space do they seem to take up?
- What sort of environment do the koa trees create around them? (dense or light shade, still or breezy, etc.)
- What disturbances are apparent? (animal or wind damage, for example)
- Are there symptoms of stress showing in the trees, such as drought stress, insect pests, etc.?

(See "Where to See Koa Trees" and "Trails and Hiking" on page 96 for some ways to experience koa, and "Rob Pacheco" on page 88 for one naturalist's observations of a koa in the forest.)

Gathering Information

Learning from the forest

Before starting the planning process for planting koa, it is very helpful to spend some time in a koa forest in order to understand the forest better. Trees in nature are connected with each other and with many communities of other organisms in ways that support long-term survival for the trees and their associates. Observing koa in nature gives clues as to how the tree can be supported, and in turn benefit other elements in the living system.

Ideally a person considering planting koa would spend some time in a koa forest in a similar ecosystem type. Find a koa tree and sit quietly. Develop a sense for some of the ecosystem processes and connections happening around the koa:

- What insects or animals can be observed in or around the koa trees?
- Are there mosses, lichens, or other plants living on the koa tree?
- What other trees or plants are thriving near the koa (in the understory, in the canopy, etc.)?
- Are the root systems bare, or covered with leaf litter?

Observing koa trees in nature helps us understand them better and better.

Learning from other people and plantings

Hawai'i is rich in people who study, perpetuate, and love koa. These include ecologists, woodworkers, foresters, traditional wood carvers, educators, cultural experts, botanists, farmers, conservationists, government agents, etc. Talk to and learn from these people. Go to conferences, field days, botanical gardens, parks and refuges where koa is planted and perpetuated.

Because Hawai'i's environments are so diverse, it is also invaluable to see any planting of koa that is nearby. These are sometimes small-scale on private property. See if there is a possibility of at least a short visit to learn about that planting's successes and challenges (see "People" on page 90 for tips about locating and approaching koa planters on private property).

Learning from the area to be planted

The site considered for planting also has a tremendous amount to offer in terms of guiding how, when, where (or if!) koa trees should be planted there. Rather than impose a preconceived idea onto the land, it is best to let the land determine the plan. Site observation is essential to the process of working with the land.

Observing the site can provide information for making appropriate management decisions

The description of site characteristics should include elevation, slope, rainfall regime, maximum length of dry season, soil analysis, wind and temperature information, and so forth. Any other information that can be obtained about the site will also be valuable, including a survey of existing vegetation, a history of land use, etc. The process of evaluating the project site can be as comprehensive as desired. Growers should allow sufficient time for this process—several months to a year is not an excessive amount of time. The time consumed by a detailed site evaluation is rewarded by more informed planning decisions.

Some information to gather about the site includes:

- Ecosystem type (lowland or upland, wet, moist, or dry)

- Native/original vegetation
- Land use history
- Existing vegetation (grass, sugarcane, overgrown exotics, etc.)
- Existing wildlife (birds, insects, feral animals)
- Rainfall
- Rainfall distribution (dry/wet seasons)
- Soil types (often there are several, can see from maps at NRCS)
- Soil test

Knowing the history of the site and the kind of native vegetation that was there before can be especially enlightening. Everywhere in Hawai'i, vegetation has been altered and changed by people through development, animal and plant introductions, and other related factors such as climate change. Historical descriptions of a region often amaze people who live or work there now.

The Planning Process

After gaining a better understanding of koa and koa forests, what others have learned, and the planting site itself, the planning process can begin.

The elements to be included in the strategic plan include the following:

Needs, desires, priorities and goals of the project These may include adding beauty, providing shade, leaving a legacy, enhancing wildlife habitat, creating meaningful and instructive family activity, improving property value, or the possibility of some commercial returns.

Existing site resources This includes any assets on the site, for example woody invasive plants that can be chipped for mulch for the koa trees, tools or machines to help with planting and maintenance, as well as the overall site qualities studied in the previous phase.

Existing human resources How much time and/or money can comfortably be spent to plant the trees? After installation, what is an affordable amount of time and money every season to maintain them? Is family or other labor available year round, weekends or perhaps only seasonally?

Physical layout (structures and roads) Once planted, koa trees will likely be there for decades. It is not advisable to have koa near water or utility lines or close to buildings, roads, or pathways. Planners should take current structures into account, and anticipate any future developments that might later injure the koa.

Animal invaders Lack of fencing is a great cause of koa tree loss. Pigs, cattle, horses, goats, and sheep all should be excluded if possible. If fencing is not feasible, planners should be prepared for vigilant animal control and high seedling losses.

A properly built and maintained fence keeps koa predators out

Site challenges Is the site very windy or dry? The need for windbreaks or irrigation should be considered in advance. Windbreaks require careful design, and usually must be planted several years in advance of the koa to be effective. On dry sites, if a permanent irrigation system will not be implemented, planners must strategize for other ways to get water to the seedlings during dry spells for the first six to twelve months of establishment.

Site preparation After the site has been inventoried, site preparation strategies should be carefully planned. Site preparation is often one of the most expensive aspects of planting trees, and should not be neglected. This involves preliminary weed control, sometimes clearing on overgrown sites. Sites with pahoehoe lava, soil compaction or hardpan may have additional preparation requirements.

Soil amendments If the soil test determined that the soil was very deficient in certain nutrients such as phosphorus, potassium, or calcium, it should be planned how and when these will be amended. As koa is a nitrogen fixing tree, nitrogen should not be amended.

Tree spacing If koa are planted in stands, the spacing and configuration of the trees are a key planning decision. There is no easy answer or simple recommendation available on this issue. In practice, koa spacing varies a great deal.

Current thinking is that close initial spacing facilitates straight form of koa trees. Close initial spacing also leads to faster canopy closure, which can reduce weeding costs. However, it is also true that koa trees in dense stands quickly become slow-growing (or even stop growing) as a result of competition with each other (Baker p. comm.). This requires "thinning" stands by removing slower or inferior trees to give more and more room for the best trees to grow. So, while close spacing may reduce weed costs, optimize form, and reduce or eliminate pruning needs, it also means the expense and labor of thinning trees after 2–5 years, and repeated thinnings until the koa trees are at a healthy final density.

Some projects plant at a very close initial spacing, as close as 4 x 4 feet (over 2,700 trees per acre or 6,670 per hectare). More commonly, wider spacing is used such as 8 x 8 (680 trees per acre or 1,680 per hectare) or 10 x 10 (435 trees per acre or 1,070 per hectare). Some projects mix koa with other tree and plant species and don't use a formal grid pattern of planting at all. The closer the initial spacing, the sooner the stand must be thinned to maximize the growth of the best koa.

Appropriate initial densities of koa trees in a stand should be considered carefully in terms of the project's goals, needs, resources, and budget. The final density after thinning is also a key issue (see "Thinning," below).

Special Landscaping Considerations Koa can be a fine landscaping, park or street tree when planted in the right place, providing shade, beauty, and enjoyment. It must be remembered in planning and placement that koa trees need a lot of room to grow. Ideally, allow a space 30–40 feet (9–12 m) in diameter per tree, away from paths, utilities, and buildings. Koa should not be planted near buildings or power lines. Koa have shallow root systems that extend in all directions very close to or on the surface of the soil. Generally, the roots extend at least as far out from the tree as the tree is tall.

Roots are very sensitive to foot traffic and repeated injuries such as these can affect tree health

Koa root systems can be aggressive, disrupting underground utility and water lines. Koa should only be planted where there

will be plenty of room for the roots and branches to reach full size. Pathways should also be planned to minimize disturbance to the koa roots, which are easily injured by continuous pedestrian or vehicular traffic. Planting from seed sources from dwarf or compact parent trees may be one way to reduce the area needed, although there is no guarantee that the offspring will be like the parents in size. Another option to consider for small spaces is koaiʻa (*Acacia koaia*), a close relative of koa with a much more compact form.

Tree count How many tree seedlings will be needed? Plantings are often done in increments, with the first increment sometimes being the smallest. The number of seedlings required per increment should be determined. Seedlings must be started in the nursery several months in advance of the planting date.

Obtaining seeds After visiting koa forests, speaking with koa planters, and observing the planting site, growers will usually have some idea of the seed sources to try on their site. Ideally seeds are obtained from nearby areas with similar rainfall and elevation, adapted to the site. Often several seed sources are tried on a small scale, and the most successful of these are outplanted in larger quantities (see "Genetic Trials" on page 23)

Desired tree characteristics Before seeds are collected, the desired characteristics of the trees should be determined. Most often, people wish to plant tall-growing trees with straight form and minimal side branching. However, landscaping purposes may prefer a wider canopy and shorter form. Sometimes these characteristics are environmental, but sometimes they are genetic. Parent trees should possess desirable traits.

Nursery The planner must decide if the project will set up its own nursery or contract with another nursery to grow the koa seedlings. Nursery work is an intensive process involving daily supervision and technical training. There are advantages to the control allowed by having a nursery on the site. Commercial nurseries are usually willing to grow from seeds provided by the customer, or may offer collection services.

Increment size For projects larger than just a few trees, planting is often done in smaller, more manageable increments. The first increment might be considered a small test plot or trial, maintained for a season or two to ensure that the strategies are well-developed and successful before expanding the planting (see "Starting Small" on page 21).

Installation/planting strategy Safe transport from the nursery to the field, planting techniques and necessary tools, initial watering and amendments if necessary, should be planned and all needed materials collected prior to planting day.

Schedule Trees are living and growing organisms, and once started from seed, their needs dictate the schedule. Timing is an essential aspect of tree planting success. Land preparation, initial weed control, nursery work, and outplanting must be carried out when needed. Areas with a pronounced dry season where there is only a small window of optimal planting weather have additional timing issues to consider. Creating a time line for development will help keep activities on track.

Weed control strategies Even on planting sites that are well prepared, weed control can be time-consuming. Mulch, herbicide, mowing and weedeating are common weed control strategies. The specifics appropriate to the site, including an anticipated schedule and frequency, should be worked out in advance. It should be noted that koa are extremely sensitive to herbicide; even a few tiny droplets touching the leaves can kill a small seedling. For this reason, alternatives to herbicide should be considered. If herbicide will be used, it must be applied with extreme care.

After 1–4 years, koa with good growth will usually provide good canopy cover and suppress most understory weeds with their shade. However, occasional weed maintenance, especially of grass and climbing vines, will help the trees to thrive.

Watering Many sites don't have the luxury of irrigation. However, in dry areas, finding a way to get young seedlings through dry spells for the first six to twelve months is important to prevent seedling mortality.

Additional fertilization There are no set formulas for if and how much of what kind of fertilizer benefit growing koa. Nitrogen fertilizer should not be used. However, the addition of phosphorus and other nutrients may aid growth.

Pruning (if absolutely necessary) Selected seed and a close spacing configuration are intended to facilitate good tree form and preclude the necessity of pruning. Most people agree that pruning koa trees is harmful, slowing growth and increasing risks of disease. However, others contend that some pruning is necessary for good tree form or ease of maintenance. If it is deemed absolutely necessary to prune, it should be done minimally and properly.

Thinning If closely planted to encourage straight stems, the koa planting will soon need to be thinned. Failure to thin will greatly reduce the growth and potential long-term values of overcrowded trees. The final number of trees per acre after thinning varies, and there are no set recommendations. Some projects plan for a final density as high as 100 koa trees per acre (250/hectare); others have 35–50 trees per acre (86–124/hectare). In natural forests there are often just a few large koa trees per acre, so some projects plan final densities as low as 4–8 large koa trees per acre (10–20/hectare). It should be noted that thinning usually occurs in increments, for example, by removing half the trees after two or four years, and continuing stand thinning until at twenty years the desired final density is achieved. (See Chapter 8, "Management" on page 57 and "Patrick Baker" on page 72 for more about thinning.)

Budget Planting and caring for koa trees costs money and time. Planning should detail anticipated costs and create a budget that is affordable. When in doubt, planners should start with a small increment and do it well rather than spread resources too thin over a larger area. Planning should also budget for early and later maintenance, keeping in mind the desired outcomes of the planting.

Good early maintenance of the understory is one key to successful establishment (pictured: Charles Anderson)

Any project with a goal of financial returns will require more intensive planning, usually in partnership with a professional forester or resource planner. Economic predictions, risk assessments, access areas for harvesting machinery, a budget for thinning and harvest activities, marketing strategies, and an environmental impact statement are just some of the elements that should be included in a commercial forestry plan. It should be noted that planting koa for commercial returns is considered a very risky investment; there are a lot of uncertainties.

Revisiting the Plan Seasonally

Feedback is an essential part of strategic planning. The plan is not a rigid document; it must respond effectively to the unpredictable nature of reality. Environmental conditions, economic circumstances, priorities, capital and labor availability, and so forth will determine what gets done and what succeeds. In addition, ongoing research generates new data and suggestions for effective koa planting and management. Work plans should be reviewed seasonally or at least annually, in order to alter the plan according to changing circumstances or priorities.

New work plans are then made, with reference to the original long-term visions and goals.

Starting Small

For any project larger than a few koa trees, starting small is a good strategy. Even large reforestation projects break the work up into smaller increments, often starting with just one to three acres (0.4–1.2 hectares) before expanding. For smaller projects with limited land and resources, starting small can be a key strategy to save money by decreasing risks and avoiding costly mistakes. For example, the first increment could be an area or tree count of 1–10% of the total to be planted. It is much better to have one small area thriving and successful than a larger area that is struggling.

It's best to start a small scale, and expand on successes

Why does it work to start small? Starting small enables the planter to:

Do it right The first few months of site preparation, outplanting, and early care will be very labor and time intensive, requiring vigilant attention and prompt management. This is not a time to be spread too thin. Once this first increment feels well in hand and isn't taking up a lot of time and effort (usually after six to twelve months), then it is appropriate to move on to the next increment.

Develop effective habits Every site is different, and as emphasized repeatedly, when it comes to koa there are a lot of unknowns and no set recommendations available for planting and management success. The person taking care of the trees will have to learn what works best on their site and with their koa as far as how and when to maintain weeds, water, fertilize, etc. On a small scale, there is time and capacity to be very observant and learn what is necessary.

Trial strategies A small-scale first increment can serve as a testing ground for various management strategies being considered. In planting koa, a person with unlimited resources could do meticulous maintenance over a large area. In the real world, most koa planters are working with very limited time and money, and so the question that comes up echoes that of the great Japanese farmer Masanobu Fukuoka, "The usual way to go about developing a method is to ask 'How about trying this?' or 'How about trying that?'... My way was opposite. 'How about *not* doing this? How about *not* doing that?'" (Fukuoka 1978). A small trial might establish if there are differences between a trial area maintained with "luxury" treatment (everything that could be done, is done) when compared to an area that, say, received a little less weed control, water, or mulch. Planters learn by observation what is the most effective thing to do and when for their particular site and work habits.

Innovate and improve Many ideas form while out in the field doing the hands-on part of the work that simply cannot be conceptualized when planning on paper. Many koa planters have developed innovative and effective techniques that work well for their particular needs while installing and maintaining the first increment. These can make the work easier and more efficient. The

benefits of these innovations apply to future increments. Each increment tends to get better and easier when a project starts small.

Learn from mistakes It is much more fun to say, "Next time we'll know..." when there is going to be a next time. Making mistakes is an essential part of the learning process. It's much more satisfying to make a mistake on a small scale, when is a learning experience. Failing on a large scale can put an end to a project and discourage everyone involved.

Many planters have spent years developing specialized and effective techniques. (pictured: Baron Horiuchi)

Create a realistic time-line and budget The first increment will clarify the kind of time and resources it takes to install and manage the trees. This knowledge enables good scheduling and budgeting for future increments. For example, perhaps the planter will discover that she or he could handle three times the expenses and labor for an increment; or, perhaps it will turn out that small increments the same size as the original trial are more comfortable.

Trial seed sources Chapter 4, "Seeds" on page 25 discusses some of the amazing genetic variability found in koa in terms of site adaptability, growth, form, and wood quality. Projects of any size should consider several seed sources and conduct a few trials to see which selections perform the best on their site. Planting an entire area without trials runs the risk of missing out on the potential benefits and diversity of seed selections that might be superior performers on that site. The section below explains a little bit how to do seed source trials.

Journal

One key aspect of benefiting from the "start small" strategy is keeping a log or journal. A few minutes spent jotting down each day in a simple calendar or log what was done, how much time and/or money was spent doing it, and any observations of how things are going will be invaluable for strategizing future increments. A few other notes, such as rainfall and weather conditions, can add to the value. Aside from its very practical and immediate benefits to evolving the strategic plan, this journal may one day be an interesting piece of history to future generations of koa lovers sitting in the shade of the trees that were planted.

Genetic Trials

There is tremendous variation in growth rates, tree form, tree size, disease susceptibility, and wood quality of different koa seed sources. These genetic variations can affect tree health and performance. For this reason, it is wise to try several different seed sources of koa to determine which are good matches for the planting site.

Ongoing research might one day be able to give tree planters "best bet" seed source recommendations for any particular site. The future might also bring improved koa that are bred and selected for different environments, such as lowland areas or *Fusarium* resistance.

In the meantime, choosing seed sources is rather experimental. Using seeds from nearby and similar environments is considered the safest bet. However, Hawai'i's many different climates and soil types can make it a challenge to match seed sources to the environment. A seed source just a few miles away from the planting site may experience dramatic differences in rainfall, soil type, cloud cover, and so forth. Offspring from a koa tree that grows well on one site may perform poorly on

another site, or it might be susceptible to certain pests and diseases. Therefore, it is best to try out several different seed selections from different sources when possible.

A tree that has survived a long time on a harsh site may be a good candidate as a seed source for similar conditions

The ideal would be to trial a number of different seed selections on the planting site for a full "rotation," that is, through to tree maturity, which in koa's case could be 25–100 years. The most reliable information comes from species trials conducted in formal, designed experiments that examine all phases of growth (MacDicken 1994).

Since this is usually not feasible, even two or three years of informal species trials is valuable. No amount of research and advice can substitute for test plantings on the intended planting site. The trial period typically involves planting seedlings from a range of seed sources. For example, one possible strategy for a small-scale informal trial is to use seeds from four different sources. One would be from a local source within 1,500 feet (460 m) elevation of the intended planting site, preferably from an area with similar soils and rainfall patterns. The other three would be seeds collected from stands in areas farther away or at higher elevations, but with similar soils and rainfall (amount and distribution throughout the year).

Even a year of trials will often indicate variation between seed sources, although long term observation is needed for definitive selections

The performance of these seed sources can then be observed. Results from such trials will not be conclusive; for example, trees still thriving after a decade of growth still might eventually succumb to *Fusarium* or some other disease (Scowcroft p. comm.). In addition, projects hoping for high quality wood might find after several decades that a seed source whose trees grew and performed well in the end yielded low density, pale colored, or otherwise lower quality wood. However, there are some early positive signs that a seed source is a good match for the site. These include (after Wadsworth 1997):

- Early height growth is a good indicator of adaptation of species to a site.
- Uniform growth of trees within a stand denotes favorable conditions.
- Self-pruning is a sign of a favorable site.
- Susceptibility to insects and diseases is minimal on sites to which trees are well adapted.

The time and expense devoted to testing candidate seed sources should be viewed as an investment in the future success of the project. Starting on a small scale and observing the results will aid in expansion to a larger scale planting. It is also an important form of risk-management, preventing growers from staking scarce time, land, and resources on selections that do not perform as expected. Two or three years of seed source trials may serve to eliminate some seed sources from the list, and narrow the candidates down to those with the greater possibility for success on the site. Future plantings can then expand on successes. However, high genetic diversity should always be maintained by planting trees from many different parents as described in the Chapter 4, "Seeds" on page 25. If a number of the trialed seed sources grow well, continuing to outplant many varieties can help insure against unforeseen future conditions by maintaining a high level of genetic diversity. For example, some of the slower-growing selections may in the end turn out to have better drought tolerance or disease resistance.

Chapter 4: Seeds

The characteristics of individual koa trees can vary dramatically. For example, there are koa trees that are small, multi-branched, and shrubby, and on the other end of the spectrum there are koa trees that are tall, with a single, straight trunk. Other variations can be found in leaf (phyllode) size and shape, seed size and shape, wood color and quality, and many other characteristics. There are also variations in growth rate, adaptation to environmental conditions such as drought or vog (volcanic smog), and resistance to diseases and pests. Most of these characteristics are genetic; they are passed from one generation to the next.

Left: **It's relatively easy to pick seeds from branchy trees;** *Right:* **It takes time, patience, and sometimes special equipment to collect seeds from tall, majestic trees like this one, but the extra effort is worth it**

People who want to strengthen and expand the presence of koa and koa forests are concerned about fostering diverse populations that are strong and well-adapted for reforestation. Because koa is prized for its wood, people also desire large koa trees with high quality wood and long, straight trunks (often called "canoe koa").

Genetic Quality

For generations, people have unwittingly been depleting the gene pool of koa by cutting down the trees with the most sought-after characteristics (especially tall form and excellent wood qualities) and leaving behind the smaller, forked or more stunted trees. While it is possible that this process may have started with the ancient practice of harvesting the most majestic koa trees for canoes, it was greatly accelerated with the advent of commercial logging and the introduction of heavy machinery. Of even higher impact is the broadscale destruction of koa forests to make way for agriculture and development, and the devastating effects of grazing cattle, sheep,

goats, and pigs. It is estimated that about 90% of the gene pool of koa has been lost. The process of depleting a species of the best genetic properties so that future populations are inferior to their ancestors is called "genetic degradation."

It is vital that koa planting efforts make strides to reverse the centuries of genetic degradation and improve the gene pool by propagating seed from carefully selected koa trees. At the same time, the practice of using select genetic material can improve the productivity and health of a koa planting. Care in selecting seed sources will foster plants that are better adapted to local site conditions and better suited to achieve the desired results. Long-term ecological viability is also at stake, as projects should ideally foster enough diversity to reproduce healthy and productive offspring for future generations.

The short and long term impacts of genetic seed quality warrant careful consideration and planning when collecting or purchasing seeds.

Obtaining seeds, whether purchased or collected, is definitely an area where "quality over quantity" has to be the standard.

Distressed and stunted trees tend to produce the most abundant seed. Likewise, trees with shrubby form, leaning or growing low to the ground are easy to access. Focusing on a single tree like this, a person could easily collect a large amount of koa seeds in a short time for a very low investment of time and care. However, collectors should *avoid* collecting from such trees, as their undesirable traits could be passed on. Collectors should instead collect from trees with the best form, vigor, and health—the offspring of such trees will tend to have similar qualities. Often the trees with the most desirable characteristics are also the most challenging to collect seed from because they are the tallest, most difficult to access, and most sparing in their seed production. However, the extra effort to collect from these parent trees is worth it.

Much of the remaining koa forest has already been harvested for its best trees

Collectors of koa seeds should adhere to strict criteria to ensure that they are perpetuating healthy, viable koa trees for the forests of the future.

Selection Criteria

Seeds that are collected from parent trees with desirable genetic traits are known as "select" seed. Such seed is selected for traits that could strengthen the health and productivity of the offspring. There are important standards to keep in mind when collecting seeds. If seeds are being purchased, the supplier should be asked if they follow these standards too.

Before collecting from an abundant seed source within hand's reach, consider if the characteristics of the tree are desirable qualities for the planting

When acquiring seeds for a koa planting, seed collectors should seek parent trees that meet the following criteria:

1 Adaptation to the site conditions. Different populations have varying tolerances to environmental conditions and stresses. A local seed source can yield trees better adapted to the site conditions including soils, wind, elevation and rainfall. For example, offspring from koa trees growing in areas subject to drought are likely to be more drought tolerant (Ares, Fownes, and Sun 2000). Trees from areas with heavy vog (volcanic fog) and the associated acid rain may be more tolerant of vog (Simmons p. comm.). When possible, seed from koa populations that are adapted to conditions similar to the site where the trees will be planted should be used.

2 Resistance to pests and diseases. Koa is susceptible to many pests and diseases. The presence of certain pests and diseases varies from site to site. A local tree that is healthy and vigorous is a good candidate as a seed

source. Seed should not be collected from any tree that shows obvious signs of pest or disease problems.

3 Tree characteristics. Tree characteristics such as form and wood quality are likely to be passed on to the offspring of a tree. Collectors should seek out parent trees that are representative of the qualities that are desirable for the project. For forestry and timber projects, straight form, a lack of low branches, and high quality wood are the most desirable characteristics. However, for landscaping uses, a smaller, more branching form might be desired.

Collecting seeds from trees with poor health or disease can increase the likelihood that the offspring will have similar problems (pictured: witches' broom)

4 Tree growth rate. Selecting seed from trees that are the best performers may achieve an increase in overall growth rate.

5 Genetic diversity of the seed. It is also essential that a koa planting contain diversity and vigor in the gene pool to protect against unforeseen biological and environmental stresses. At a minimum, seeds should be collected from at least 30 individual trees. To reduce the chance of collecting from closely related individuals, seeds should be collected from trees separated by 200 feet (70 meters) or more (Dawson and Were 1998). Seeds should be picked from throughout the canopy of each tree to ensure that a range of pollinators is represented in the seeds. No one tree should be over-represented; pick similar quantities

of seeds from each tree. This helps prevent inbreeding in future generations. For projects where only a few koa seedlings will be grown, it is still best to collect from at least three parent trees. Seeds should be collected from wild stands. Koa plantings done by people in the past may have too narrow a genetic base to be a viable source of seed, and the offspring of such populations may be inbred. Collectors must also be sure to leave plenty of seed on the tree in the wild to allow that population to regenerate naturally.

Picking

Koa produces pods about 6 inches (15 cm) long and 1–1.5 inches (2–4 cm) wide. The pods are ready to pick when they turn brown, and when opened the seeds inside are deep brown and full (not green, flat, or small).

Before collecting seeds from any koa tree, be sure to have permission from the landowner or appropriate government agency. The Hawaiian way is also to ask permission (silently from the heart, or aloud) from the land and from the tree itself prior to collection, and to thank the tree after. While cynics may have their doubts, many people agree that integrity and respect for nature is an essential foundation of any undertaking, especially planting trees.

Clean healthy seeds

Once permission is granted, dry pods can be picked by hand from the tree. It should be done carefully to avoid damaging the branch. For tall trees, collecting dry seed pods from the ground is sometimes easiest. Where that is not fruitful, special equipment must be used to gain access to the canopy.

Drying

Once collected, pods should be dried in the sun just enough to make them "crunchy" when pressed in the hand. It's important not to leave the pods in the heat of the sun too long, however; too much exposure to temperatures over 95°F (35°C) can reduce viability of koa seeds. Once the pods are dry enough, they will open easily. At that point, individual seeds can be extracted by opening pods up by hand, or, for larger quantities, by machine threshing. Because seed size varies, a pound of processed koa seeds can contain as few as 2,500 seeds up to over 7,500 seeds, depending on seed size.

Well-dried seed pods are easy and fun to clean (pictured: Anya Tagawa and Cynthia Thurkins)

Once out of the pods, the seeds themselves may require a little more drying. The dryness of the seed is a major concern if seed will be stored; if seed will be used immediately, it is not all that important. Low moisture content is essential for long-term storage—the lower the moisture content, the longer the life of the seeds will be. Generally, a moisture content of 6–8% is desirable. Seeds that are dried below 4% moisture can be injured by over drying (Thomson and Stubsgaard 1998). If seeds are

purchased, they usually come with a moisture content in the 6–8% range. If seeds are collected, it is more difficult to judge the moisture content of seeds without special equipment or laboratory procedures. As a very general rule, dry the seeds to a hardness where an indentation no longer appears when the seed is pressed with a thumbnail.

Storage

The dried seeds should be stored in a cool, dry place out of direct sunlight. The two most significant factors which effect long term viability of seeds are the moisture content of the seeds and the temperature of storage.

Use airtight containers for seed storage. Label the seed source and date collected.

Properly dried seeds with a low moisture content must be stored in airtight containers, or they will slowly absorb moisture from the air. Suitable containers include glass, plastic or metal containers that have an airtight seal. Standard plastic bags allow moisture vapor to pass through them, and are unsuitable for storing seeds for long periods.

After moisture, temperature is the second most important factor effecting seed longevity in storage. When properly dried, koa seeds store for about 12–24 months at room temperature. Cooler conditions will prolong viability. Assuming the seeds are well dried, storage temperature of less than 40°F (5°C) down to 0°F (–18°C) are ideal. In these conditions, koa seeds can remain viable in storage for many years.

Chapter 5: Nursery Practices

Koa is a relatively easy-to-propagate species. It is capable of growing in a wide variety of nursery conditions and container types. As such, the subject of nursery practices for koa has perhaps not received as much attention as it deserves in order to facilitate optimum growth and productivity in the field.

Whether a project grows its own trees or acquires them from a nursery, the quality of the seedlings is vital to the success of the project.

What is a high quality seedling? There are two main factors in gauging seedling quality: the genetic make-up of the parent stock, and the physical characteristics of the seedling. Genetics were discussed in the previous chapter; it is essential that seeds from a diversity of carefully selected parent trees are used. This chapter introduces some of the nursery practices that lead to a strong seedling.

Growing high quality koa seedlings requires investment in infrastructure, materials, labor, training, and time. But the potential benefits of good nursery practices far outweigh their costs. Compared to the expense of land preparation, planting, and maintenance, the expense of seedlings is usually a small fraction of the total investment in planting koa. However, high quality koa seedlings can achieve better growth, have a higher survival rate, and also provide a faster and higher return of the desired products or services of the tree, whether those are shade and beauty, wood production, wildlife habitat, land restoration, or other goals.

In contrast, lax efforts towards seedling quality can result in lost opportunity throughout the life of the tree (Jones 2001). Low-quality seedlings will experience slower growth after transplanting and add to the

The goal is to create healthy, vigorous seedlings capable of thriving in the field. *Top:* Open pasture; *Bottom:* Three year-old trees (pictured: Charles Anderson)

costs of weed control and maintenance. Because koa is shade-intolerant, weeds may overtake a slow-growing young seedling and shade it out entirely, thwarting its growth or leading to its decline. Weaker trees may have lower product yields, and be less able to resist disease and insects.

Good nursery practices will create vigorous, sturdy, healthy koa seedlings with a maximized capacity to survive and thrive in the field. Aside from good genetics, targets include sturdy, upright stems, well-formed, hardy root systems, and a good root-to-shoot ratio. Optimally, nursery practices can also foster natural partnerships between the koa seedlings and beneficial soil microbial partners including rhizobia bacteria and mycorrhizal fungi that will support the seedlings' independence, growth and survival in the field.

There are a number of steps that can be taken to ensure that seedlings will be as healthy and productive as possible. These apply regardless of the size of the project, whether just a few trees or many thousands.

General Nursery Set-Up

The nursery area for koa seedlings should have access to water and full sunlight. It should also be protected from animals as much as possible: rodents and some birds will eat koa seeds and germinants, and livestock will eat seedlings. Ideally, koa seedlings are best grown on raised benches at least 18 inches (46 cm) off the ground, to help prevent soil pathogens from reaching the potting media. Most importantly, the nursery should be close to people so that the seedlings can receive daily attention and care until they are ready to be planted in the field.

Containers

When people think of growing plants in containers, they often picture the foliage and stems. However, growing koa seedlings should be thought of predominantly in terms of the roots. The ability of a tree seedling's root system to grow out into the surrounding soil with vigor and good form after outplanting is directly related to the growth and survival of the tree seedlings in the field (Landis et al 1990). Poor root systems can cause a seedling to grow slowly, and structural problems in the roots can lead to health and survival problems later.

For small forestry seedlings, tubes or open-ended suspended pots are usually used. These have ribbing on the sides to train the roots to grow without spiraling or wrapping around each other.

Grown in forestry tube containers, koa seedlings are usually about eight inches (20 cm) tall and well-rooted for transplanting within 12–18 weeks, depending on the size of the container, the ambient temperature of the

nursery, and the time of year. It is important to transplant the seedlings when they are ready. Even in root training containers, seedlings can become rootbound, slowing or stagnating growth.

Forestry containers usually have an open end where roots are air-pruned

For one gallon and larger containers, care must be taken that the container facilitates good root form. The round, smooth-walled pots that are the standard in the ornamental nursery trade are designed for foliage or flowers. In such containers, once the koa seedling's roots come in contact with the side of the container, they are directed down or sideways, and begin to circle the pot. When such a seedling is transplanted in the field, the root spiraling can lead to strangulation as the tree grows, or to toppling in a high wind.

A healthy koa grown in a two-gallon poly bag

There are a number of special root-training container systems available for one-gallon and larger sized root systems that preclude spiraling. These containers, like the forestry tubes, have ribbing and/or other root training and air root pruning systems that support healthy root structure.

Examples of root training one gallon containers which support healthy root structure (pictured: a RootMaker® (Whitcomb system) and a Tall One Treepot®)

For noncommercial koa plantings, if it is not feasible to acquire special root-training container systems for larger seedlings, polyethylene bags (black plastic bags) may be used. These do not prevent root spiraling, but they are low-cost and considered a better choice than hard-sided round pots (Whitcomb 1988).

Regardless of the container type used, it will be crucial to watch the seedlings closely and outplant as soon as they are sizable.

Potting Media

As a widely adapted pioneer species, koa seedlings are capable of growing in a variety of potting media. For a small scale or noncommercial planting, most commercially available potting media can be used in the nursery, mixed with less expensive materials such as cinder if desired.

Optimal potting media have special qualities as listed below

For larger-scale plantings, health and performance can be enhanced by mixing specialized potting mixes. A basic, well-drained mix of peat and perlite (usually at a ratio of one part peat to one part perlite) can serve as a base. For optimum seedling health, nursery potting media for koa has the following characteristics:

- well-drained
- balanced pH
- composed of clean and pre-sterilized materials (to avoid introducing diseases)
- does not contain nitrogen fertilizer (if inoculated with rhizobia, see below) or high amounts of phosphorus (if inoculated with mycorrhizal fungi, see below)
- contains potassium, calcium, and magnesium, as well as micronutrients including iron and molybdenum
- contains endomycorrhizal inoculant (see next section for explanation)

Mycorrhizal Fungi

Mycorrhizal fungi form a symbiotic association with many kinds of plants and trees, acting as a kind of conduit for nutrients from the soil to the root. Eighty to ninety percent of the world's plant families associate with mycorrhizal fungi, including koa and many of its forest associates such as 'ōhi'a lehua (*Metrosideros polymorpha*). The association is known to improve nutrient uptake, particularly of phosphorus, but also of micronutrients such as zinc and copper (Habte 2001).

With the help of mycorrhizal fungi, a seedling can often take up many times more of certain nutrients than would be possible in the absence of the fungi. Mycorrhizal associations can also improve a tree's drought resistance, salt tolerance, and resistance to soil pathogens and adverse conditions prevailing on degraded lands. Research with mycorrhizal inoculant and koa has established that inoculation does have a beneficial effect on early tree establishment, giving the trees a "jumpstart" in their early growth (Miyasaka p. comm.).

Erosion, soil disturbance, flooding, and the use of pesticides and fumigants diminish the presence of indigenous mycorrhizal fungi spores in the soil. The use of mycorrhizal inoculants is becoming standard in forestry and conservation nurseries, but until recently their use has been very limited in Hawai'i. However, there are a number of commercial sources now available in the state, which can be added to the potting media. Quality of these can be extremely variable, so it is important to seek out a reliable source that is tested for high spore count. Researchers at the University of Hawai'i have also developed a low-input method for nurseries to make their own highly effective crude mycorrhizal inoculant (Habte 2001). Because inoculants come in so many forms, discussing the application of each is beyond the scope of this book. In general they are incorporated into the potting media. An excess of phosphorus in the fertilizer will inhibit the partnership from taking effect.

Getting Seeds to Sprout (Scarification)

Koa seeds have a hard outer layer that is normally impenetrable to water. Koa seed can remain dormant for decades, not absorbing water even in moist or water-logged conditions. To hasten germination, the hard outer layer should be treated to allow water to penetrate into the germ so the seed can sprout.

The process of breaking the seed coat so the seed can sprout is known as "scarification." When scarified correctly, the seeds will germinate uniformly and quickly, usually within just 2–7 days from treatment. If the seeds are not scarified, they will germinate unevenly over months or even years.

In nature, hard seeds are scarified in several ways, including abrasion against rocks in the soil, exposure to high temperatures, or passing through the digestive tract of an animal. By remaining dormant until environmental events such as landslides, erosion, or fire occur, seeds with hard seed coats like koa are ready to germinate and recolonize damaged land.

On large scale projects where there are viable koa seeds in the soil, this process is sometimes mimicked by lightly scraping the soil surface with a bulldozer. This is called "scarifying the site." However, bulldozing only works for projects where there are viable koa seeds in the soil. Even then, involving a bulldozer for broadscale site scarification may not be desirable due to economic and environmental drawbacks.

For seeds to be sown in nursery conditions, nature's means of scarification can be simulated by several methods. When done properly, scarification results in a uniform and high level of germination. However, if done improperly, scarifying can harm or kill the seeds, so caution is advised. It is a good idea to scarify and germinate one or two small test batches of a seed lot to make sure the technique is working before treating a large amount of seed.

Mechanical scarification method

The seed coat can be nicked by hand using a nail clipper, file, knife, or even sand paper. This is called "mechanical scarification." A nail clipper is the safest and most effective tool.

Scarified seeds soaking in glass of water

Hand nicking with a nail clipper is a very efficient way to scarify small numbers of seeds

The idea is to nick the seed coat just enough to allow water to penetrate without damaging the plant tissues. To avoid damaging the cotyledons and embryo, seeds are nicked on the side or end opposite the point of attachment to the pod. Nick the seed just enough to break through the outer seed coat. It is surprising how effective a shallow nick can be. In fact, the shallower a seed can be nicked, the better. Be sure not nick into the germ, as this can damage the cotyledons (young leaves), allow rot or disease to enter the seed, and may even kill the seed.

Seeds that are scarified will take on water after being soaked overnight. *Left:* Not scarified, did not take on water; *Middle:* Slight nick, took on water, ready to plant; *Right:* Seed took on water but was damaged because nicked too deeply

Left: A perfect shallow nick. *Right:* A deep gouge that did too much damage

After nicking, soaking the seeds in clean, room temperature water overnight hastens germination. After soaking, the scarified seed will swell with water, ready to sprout.

If the seed does not take on water after 12–24 hours of soaking, the seed coat was not nicked deeply enough during scarification. Seeds can be nicked again and the soaking process repeated. If the seed was nicked too deeply, the damage will be more obvious when it has swelled with water.

Seeds that are mechanically scarified germinate quickly, often within in 2–7 days. Because mechanical nicking is very labor intensive, it is most practical to use it for small seed lots. However, because koa seeds are a precious resource, this technique is also used on a large scale in nurseries as well.

A properly nicked seed will germinate within 2–7 days

Hot water method

Exposing seeds briefly to hot water is a common method for scarifying large quantities of seeds. Hot water exposure for too long or too high of a temperature can easily kill koa seeds, so extreme caution is advised. It is recommended to pour near boiling water (195°F, 90°C) over the seeds and let them soak for one minute. The volume ratio should be 5–10 parts water to one part seeds. The seeds are stirred continually during the one minute hot water bath. After the hot water exposure time has elapsed, cool water is stirred in to immediately reduce the heat and prevent the seeds from being "cooked." The seeds are then soaked in cool water overnight.

the waxy coating has been dissolved. Once the seeds have become uniformly dull, but not pitted, the acid is poured off, and the seeds are rinsed well in clean water for a few minutes. Water must never be added to or spilled into concentrated sulfuric acid. The acid can be reused 2–3 times. Seeds germinate in 2–10 days. As with other methods, acid can kill if in contact with the seeds too long. Test batches should be done for each new seed lot. Acid treatment is a dangerous and unpleasant process, and not usually recommended.

Pouring near-boiling water over the seeds is an easy and common method to scarify koa seeds

Seeds that have taken on water during soaking are ready to germinate

The seeds that have taken on water after a night of soaking were successfully scarified. The seeds that did not absorb water after overnight soaking were not scarified and need to be treated again.

Seeds germinate sporadically over 5–10 days, sometimes longer.

Concentrated acid treatment

Handling concentrated acid is extremely dangerous and should be done only in laboratories by skilled technicians. This method requires concentrated sulfuric acid (93–98%), laboratory equipment, safety equipment, and laboratory training. Seeds are soaked in acid so that they are just visible below the liquid's surface. Soaking time is 10–60 minutes. The duration of soaking is judged by the appearance of the seeds. As the acid acts, the seed coats turn from shiny to dull, indicating

Sowing

Once the scarified koa seeds have absorbed water (after 12–24 hours of soaking), they are ready to plant. It is recommended to sow scarified seeds that have taken on water directly into the growing container. Cover with potting mix shallowly, about 1/4 inch (0.6 cm) deep (about as deep as the seed is wide). Water well with a fine-headed sprayer, and keep watered daily during germination. Koa seedlings will germinate in the dark or in full light. However, outdoors they will need to be protected from seed predators including mice, rats, and cardinals, as well as from hard rains that might wash out the seeds. Keeping them in a greenhouse or under other temporary cover can accomplish this, with seedlings moved to full sun conditions after a week or two.

An Ancient Partnership: Rhizobia Bacteria and Koa

Certain soil microorganisms evolved in partnership with koa and remain essential to koa's growth and health. One of these is a soil bacteria called *Bradyrhizobium* bacteria (rhizobia for short).

Chapter 2 discusses that koa is a nitrogen-fixing tree, and that it fixes nitrogen through a partnership with rhizobia bacteria. Although the terms "nitrogen fixing plants" and "nitrogen fixing trees (NFTs)" are widely used, the plants themselves do not have the ability to make use of the nitrogen gas in the air—it is only through the symbiotic association with rhizobia that the process takes place. Rhizobia live in nodules on the root systems of koa trees. The rhizobia are able to "fix" or gather nitrogen from the air and make it available to their tree host. The tree provides energy to feed the bacteria and fuel the nitrogen fixation process. In return, the bacteria hosted in the nodules provide the plant with nitrogen for growth. The koa tree and the rhizobia are partners in a symbiotic relationship.

Restoring the Partnership

Many koa planters have a larger vision for their project than simply creating a stand of trees: they want their trees to survive independently, and to reestablish some of the ecosystem value of a forest. The process of biological nitrogen fixation depends on the koa tree forming a partnership with an effective rhizobia strain. However, as koa trees have been removed from the landscape through deforestation or development, the bacteria population that lived on the koa roots has also dwindled in the soil. Today, as koa trees are planted on old sugar cane land, degraded pasture, in landscapes and other areas that have not been in koa forest for decades or even centuries, the low presence or viability of the rhizobia population may delay or compromise the seedling's ability to form the partnership. Researchers have also found that over a period of years, rhizobia in the soil can and do lose the ability to fix nitrogen (Keyser p. comm.).

Heavily cultivated and eroded lands may have low numbers or viability of beneficial microlife, including rhizobia

In many cases in Hawai'i, koa seedlings often form a partnership with some kind of rhizobia strain eventually. If rhizobia populations in the soil are low or inactive, it can take months or even two to three years for the rhizobia partnership to form (Scowcroft, p. comm.). Without their rhizobia partnership, koa trees are as dependent as any non-nitrogen fixing tree on nitrogen fertilizer inputs. Koa trees that have not formed the partnership or are not frequently fertilized will grow very slowly, often out-competed by grasses or weeds. With the partnership, koa can accumulate nitrogen for its own growth, and eventually contribute fertility to the land.

Rhizobia Strains

There are numerous strains or types of rhizobia bacteria. Some rhizobia strains are optimal partners for koa, providing abundant nitrogen at a low cost to the tree. Other strains are mediocre or poor providers of nitrogen, but require a lot of energy from the tree. In Hawai'i, the effectiveness of the many different rhizobia strains is highly variable. In addition, many Hawaiian soils have exotic rhizobia strains that will partner with koa, but are not ideal partners for koa (Keyser p. comm.).

Left: An uninoculated seedling only a few feet tall after three years of growth, requiring high maintenance; *Right:* On the same site, inoculated seedlings from select seed grew 8–12 feet (2.4–3.6 m) in just one year (pictured: Desmond Twigg-Smith)

Whether a koa will promptly and spontaneously associate with an optimal rhizobia partner in the field depends on if the site has the right strain of bacteria present, healthy, and active in the soil. Introducing the correct rhizobia strains into the potting media of young koa seedlings in the nursery can restore this partnership. This ensures that the seedlings are actively fixing nitrogen before they go out in the field.

What Are Inoculants?

Bacterial "inoculants" are live rhizobia cultures that are applied to seeds or young seedlings, imparting the beneficial bacteria to the plant's root system.

Using rhizobia inoculants ensures that the correct rhizobia strain associates with the koa seedling, and also that the association forms very early in the tree's life to accelerate its growth and establishment.

Purpose of Inoculant

Any site that has not had koa forest for many years (which includes most pastoral and agricultural lands) may have low or inactive populations of koa rhizobia. Neglecting to inoculate koa seedlings means that the trees have to fend for themselves to form this partnership. That may take from several months to several years. In the meantime, the seedlings are dependent on inputs of nitrogen fertilizers in order to grow. The cost of buying and applying fertilizer must be covered by the tree planter, an unnecessary expense when this natural process could perform the same service.

These 8-week old flats of koa are identical, except that the tray on the right was inoculated when two weeks old and the tray on the left was not (no nitrogen fertilizer was applied to either)

If koa seedlings are being planted on land that is currently in koa forest (for example, enrichment plantings for native forests), then there is likely an active population of rhizobia already on the site. Even so, it may still be a good idea to inoculate seedlings in the nursery, as the benefits of the rhizobia association are apparent after 4–6 weeks, long before seedlings are outplanted.

The natural nitrogen fixation process provides a steady supply of nitrogen for the tree's growth, instead of spurts of soluble fertilizers. This nitrogen is available to the koa tree, but not immediately available to competing weeds and vegetation. Inoculated trees may grow faster. Faster early growth also means faster shading of understory and quicker canopy closure, which reduces weed control expenses. Inoculating tree seedlings in the nursery stage can save money in establishment of trees, and at the same time reduce the use of some chemical fertilizers and herbicides. Using rhizobia inoculants can help make it more sustainable and affordable to plant koa.

In the nursery, using inoculants means the koa in the nursery do not require nitrogen fertilizer additions, reducing pollution from nitrates.

Acquiring inoculant

There are two forms of rhizobia inoculant that can be used: manufactured inoculant, and homemade (often called "crude") inoculant.

inoculant can be obtained, it is easy to use and highly effective. Select strains of rhizobia may be as important as select seed. Select rhizobia are optimal partners for the species they were selected for, providing an abundant and steady supply of nitrogen at a low cost to the tree.

Once some of inoculated koa seedlings are on hand, nodules from their roots can serve as the basis for making crude inoculant in the future, so manufactured inoculant does not have to be purchased repeatedly.

Two sources of inoculant for koa: *Left*: Packet of manufactured inoculant; *Right*: Nodules from a koa seedling

Manufactured inoculants consist of a carrier such as finely ground peat, saturated with specific, selected strains of live rhizobia matched for koa. A mix of rhizobia strains highly effective for koa was developed by the University of Hawai'i—Nitrogen Fixation for Tropical Agricultural Legumes Project (NifTAL). This rhizobia bacteria comes in a peat-based inoculant, with billions of cells per gram. One hundred grams of inoculant is usually sufficient to inoculate up to 3000 seedlings.

Because they contain living cultures of bacteria, manufactured inoculants are perishable, and care should be taken to keep inoculants in a cool and dark place in an airtight container. The cost is very small per plant inoculated—a few dollars worth of inoculant can replace a hundred or more dollars worth of nitrogen fertilizer over the life of the tree. If select manufactured

Top: Picking off nodules; *Bottom*: Nodules gathered from healthy koa root systems

Nodules are the small root structures that house the rhizobia bacteria. When rhizobia are present and nitrogen is being fixed, nodules can be seen on the roots of the plants. Each one of the nodules can house millions of rhizobia bacteria. When a nodule is opened, a pink or red color inside is a good indicator that it is active, that biological nitrogen fixation is taking place. By blending nodules in clean water, the bacteria are suspended in a solution that can be used to inoculate. It is best to use nodules from seedlings that were inoculated with select rhizobia inoculant. However, sometimes rhizobia bacteria from the field may be the only source available. Because the strain of rhizobia bacteria from the field is unknown, homemade inoculant from field nodules may be an inferior to selected manufactured inoculant.

Preparing crude inoculant from nodules

The steps for making crude inoculant from field or nursery nodules are as follows:

1 Find a stand of koa trees near the project site. If there is a source of trees or nursery seedlings that were inoculated with select manufactured inoculant, use them, because the rhizobia are probably a superior strain. If using nursery stock, skip to step 5.

2 If in the field, search around the root system of the koa tree. Carefully lifting up rocks is a low-impact way to get to roots without digging or damaging the tree.

3 Find some nodules on the roots.

4 Open up a few nodules with a fingernail to test them. A red or pink color inside is desired; that means the rhizobia are active. If the nodules are green inside, do not use them.

Blending nodules

5 Carefully collect some nodules. Use care not to damage the koa roots—remember, they are very sensitive. For the tree's sake, nodules should be picked off cleanly, not scratched or stripped off the roots. The nodules can be placed into a sealed container or plastic bag. To inoculate 100

seedlings, about 10–20 active nodules are needed. If possible, collect nodules from several koa trees.

6 During transport, keep the collected nodules in the shade and cool. Exposure to direct sunlight can kill the rhizobia bacteria.

7 As soon as possible after collection (within a few hours), put the nodules in a blender with clean, chlorine-free water (use filtered or bottled water if available; if not, set clean water out in an open container overnight the night before to allow most of the chlorine to evaporate).

8 The homemade liquid inoculant is ready to use.

Preparing manufactured inoculant

Most manufactured inoculants are peat based, and tend to form clumps when added to water. Clumps hinder the bacteria from being distributed evenly so it is a good practice to mix the solution in a blender to break up the clumps. If a blender is not available, a whisk or a mortar and pestle can be used. If the water contains chlorine, let the water stand overnight to allow the chlorine to evaporate before adding the bacteria.

Blending a pack of manufactured inoculant

A good amount of inoculant to use is about 0.2–0.4 ounce (5–10 grams) of manufactured inoculant or 50–100 nodules per liter of water, which can be used to inoculate about 500 seedlings. This amount will usually exceed the recommended 100,000 bacteria per seedling, which allows for spillage and other losses.

Applying inoculant

Inoculation (infecting the plant roots with the rhizobia bacteria) should take place as early in the seedling's life as possible, when the plant will most readily form the association. In nursery conditions, rhizobia is commonly applied when seedlings are two weeks old.

The one liter of liquefied inoculant made from either nodules or manufactured inoculant as per the instructions above is diluted in more water (usually the liter of concentrated inoculant is poured into about 5–10 liters of water) and then soaked in to the potting media of the seedling.

Whether using homemade inoculant (left) or manufactured inoculant (right), the application is the same: simply water into two-week old seedlings

Verifying the rhizobia partnership

It takes about two to six weeks for the partnership to form noticeably. The most obvious sign that nitrogen fixation has begun is that the seedlings begin to grow vigorously and turn deep green despite the absence of added nitrogen fertilizers.

Also, the process of nitrogen fixation gives off a faint but distinctive ammonia-like scent. This is the same scent people commonly notice under other nitrogen-fixing trees, such as monkeypod.

Another indicator that the bacteria have infected (inoculated) the roots of the plant is the presence of nodules on the root system. After four to six weeks, small nodules should appear on the root system. When a nodule is opened, a pink or red color inside indicates that nitrogen fixation is taking place.

Top: Nodulating trees have a particular smell (pictured: Kira Gerrits and Sara Conti); *Bottom:* Active nodules show reddish pigment inside

Troubleshooting inoculation

In most cases following the above steps will lead to a successful partnership between koa and rhizobia. However, if after four to six weeks seedlings appear stunted or yellowish, this may indicate inoculation was unsuccessful. There are a number of possible reasons and solutions for this:

1 Failure of inoculation; i.e., the seedlings are not benefiting from nitrogen fixation. Solution: reapply inoculant. If nodules were used, perhaps find a different source.

2 The nutrients essential for nodulation and nitrogen fixation are in short supply. Solution: get a soil test, and if necessary add calcium, potassium, or micronutrients

including molybdenum and iron. Adding any missing micronutrients will usually suffice.

It's usually very easy to see when seedlings have been successfully inoculated (right side)

3 The potting medium has poor drainage, or there is too much water for the seedlings. Solution: amend watering practices, or start again with well-drained potting medium.

4 If the trees are deep green but there is no sign of nodules, there may be too much nitrogen fertilizer in the potting medium. If nitrogen fertilizer is readily available, koa will exploit that, rather than forming the partnership. Solution: flush the fertilizer out of the mix, and re-inoculate.

5 If the seedlings were inoculated when they were older than 2 weeks, the partnership will take longer (often 8–12 weeks) to form. Solution: have patience.

Once the partnership is formed, the rhizobia will survive and multiply on the root system as the koa tree grows

Nursery Care

Watering

Seedlings need adequate water. This may sound simple, but in reality ensuring that each seedling gets enough water without overwatering can be a challenge. A day or two of insufficient water can undo all the work done to this point, and throw off outplanting schedules for the season.

Seedlings must never be allowed to dry out. Any seedling that is allowed to dry out or begin to wilt because of water stress is damaged by it.

A gentle, fine-headed sprayer should be used as the seedlings germinate and until they are about two to four weeks old. At this young stage, they will probably need water daily. Thereafter, a slightly less fine spray of water can be used.

A gentle spray is best

The water needs of the koa seedlings do not conform to a regular schedule. As the seedlings grow bigger, they use more and more water. Water requirements also vary on a day by day basis; a cool or misty day will greatly reduce the water needs, while a hot sunny day will increase them. Some days seedlings may not require water; other days they made need to be watered twice. Rather than creating a strict water schedule, it works better to cultivate a feel for the watering needs of the seedlings.

When watering, the water should be soaked all the way through the root systems until water drips out the bottom. One thorough soaking is much better than more frequent shallow waterings that don't reach the bottom of the container.

Watering should ideally be done in the early morning, not in the heat of the day (unless it is an emergency). Late afternoon waterings may also not be advisable because the foliage is wet into the night, creating a welcoming environment for fungal pathogens.

With the unacceptable consequences of inadequate watering, the temptation may be to go to the other extreme and overwater seedlings. Overwatering, however, which involves keeping the root systems constantly soaked, drives the supply of necessary oxygen from the root zone, encouraging root rot.

Even in areas where the watering is automated, a human being supervising when the system turns on and when to leave it off will help prevent problems with over or under watering.

Fertilizing seedlings in the nursery

For seedlings grown in forestry tubes that started with a good potting media with sufficient nutrients (potassium, calcium, magnesium, sulfur, iron, molybdenum, etc.) and were inoculated with rhizobia bacteria and mycorrhizal fungi, fertilization will not be necessary during the nursery period of 12–18 weeks of growth before outplanting.

However, if for some reason seedlings were not inoculated with rhizobia bacteria and/or mycorrhizal fungi, then fertilization will be necessary. If it is known in advance that inoculants will not be used, then a slow-release balanced fertilizer with N, P, and K should be incorporated in the mix. If, however, the lack of inoculation was unforeseen, for example due to an unsuccessful attempt at inoculation, then liquid fertilizer may need to be added to the nursery water on a regular basis (daily or weekly) until the trees are reinoculated.

If fertilizing tree seedlings, the goal is not to produce maximum growth, but optimum growth. Unbalanced or excessive fertilization can cause seedlings to shoot up, gaining more height and foliage than stem caliper or roots. This leads to a water-demanding, top-heavy plant that may dry out rapidly or lean over when outplanted. In contrast, a balanced, conservative fertilization regime containing sufficient phosphorus for good stem development (if mycorrhizal fungi inoculant was not used), and just enough nitrogen to encourage growth but not excessive shooting

(if rhizobia inoculant was not used), and careful supervision to make sure the seedlings are healthy but not growing too fast, is effective.

Early seedling care

While koa seeds will sprout in shady or even dark conditions, koa seedlings require full sunlight to thrive. In the shade, koa seedlings will soon become spindly and stunted. It is essential that koa seedlings receive the maximum amount of sunlight possible. If they are germinated in a greenhouse, they can be moved outside at two weeks of age.

To reduce shading, it is important not to overcrowd the seedlings in the nursery. Overcrowded seedlings may shoot up as they compete for light, becoming too tall in relation to the strength of their stems. Tall, thin-stemmed seedlings are top-heavy and may bend over.

Great care should be taken to keep seedlings spaced well apart from each other to maximize light infiltration (pictured: Carlos Valdovinos)

Seedlings should be widely spaced so each tree gets a maximum amount of sunlight. This often means that seedlings need to be moved further apart from each other as they grow larger.

Water as needed. Again, it is of paramount importance that seedlings are never allowed to dry out. However, they should also not be overwatered or kept in a constant water-logged condition.

Other activities managing the seedlings include weeding if necessary, monitoring seedling health and development, and watching out for any pests or diseases.

Culling

After about 6–10 weeks of growth, most of the seedlings will be thriving. However, some of them will clearly be undersized or weak. For an average seed lot, about ten percent of the seedlings are like this, although it may be more or less.

It is not a good idea to keep these underdeveloped seedlings longer and try to nurse them along with extra care. Whatever the reason for their inadequacies, whether genetic or environmental, it not recommended to try to correct it or hold koa seedlings back for extra time. Instead, it is necessary to "cull" or remove the smallest and weakest seedlings. It is easier and cheaper to cull the poorest seedlings at this point, rather than maintain them longer in the nursery and then struggle with them (likely to no avail) after the expense of outplanting them.

It is disrespectful to send a koa seedling to a landfill. Unless they are diseased, culled seedlings can be disposed of by composting them in a garden or farm area so they can go back into the earth.

Hardening off

When the time to transplant is about four to six weeks away, it is time to "harden off" the seedlings. This means preparing them or "toughening them up" for the harsher conditions of the field. While they are already in full sun, further spacing may help maximize the sunlight and wind each tree receives. Also, watering should be reduced. The trees still must receive adequate water. This is very important. Tree roots should never be allowed to dry out, and the foliage should never show any signs of wilting; if they do, the seedling is irreparably damaged. Hardening off involves gently introducing the seedlings to moderate,

temporary water stress. This is done by reducing the frequency of watering, while still supplying plenty of water as needed.

Nursery Pests and Diseases

Good nursery pest management involves making sure the seedlings are in optimum health, protected from predators, and that the nursery is clean and free of weeds.

Koa seeds are subject to predation from a variety of creatures, including mice, rats, and some birds including cardinals. If rodents or cardinals are present, it may be necessary to protect the germinating seedlings until they are large enough to be unattractive as seed snacks. If the nursery is in an extremely dry area, rats may strip bark on older seedlings.

Koa is a hardy tree and while there are many pests and diseases that can affect it, few of these are common in the nursery. Some of the most damaging potential pests are reported here.

Left: Twig borer damage on a 4 month old seedling; *Right:* Broken stem showing active twig borers

The most serious potential nursery pest or disease is probably *Fusarium* root rot. *Fusarium* species are fungi that attack germinating seedlings, causing what's known as "damping off." When the roots of affected seedlings are examined, the cortex (outer tissue layer of the root) strips away easily, revealing brown, decaying tissue. *Fusarium* can spread rapidly from seedling to seedling, carried in spores by wind or water. *Fusarium* fungi is a high risk if soil is introduced to the potting media, or it may also be brought in on the seeds. Maintaining a high level of cleanliness during propagation can usually keep *Fusarium* from entering the nursery, and proper management including avoiding overwatering will also help. Mycorrhizal inoculation may also be antagonistic to some root pathogens (Habte 2001).

In some areas, koa seedlings are also subject to attack by borers such as the black twig borer (*Xylosandrus compactus*). These tiny insects bore a hole into the stem of seedlings, usually after the stem becomes woody. The foliage of affected seedlings will start to wilt as if they are dry; close examination of the stem will reveal the tiny hole made by the borer. After a few days, the seedling above the borer hole will be dead. There is no known remedy for this pest. Making sure to outplant seedlings when they are ready, rather than keeping woody seedlings in the nursery, is recommended.

Other common pests or diseases observed on koa seedlings are usually minor and can often be diagnosed and treated if caught early enough, such as mites or aphids. For more regarding pests and diseases, see Chapter 9, "Management."

Left: Typical mite symptoms; *Right:* Detail view of spider mite-damaged curled leaves

Timing

Timing is essential in fostering seedlings with optimal health. The length of time it will take for a koa to grow from seed to field-ready seedling varies depending on nursery conditions, environment, and management practices. In forestry-size tubes, this is usually 12–18 weeks. Koa grown in one gallon containers are usually ready in about 18–20 weeks, although this too will depend on nursery conditions and the weather. The nursery manager must be vigilant about seedling development to ensure that seedlings are transplanted at the best time, when they are sizable and growing vigorously.

Top: Rootbound seedling (note brown instead of white color of roots); *Bottom*: Healthy seedling's root system, ready for field planting

Nursery work must therefore be integrated in the overall management plan of the koa planting. In many areas of Hawai'i, the planting season is limited. For example, in drier areas, the safest time to plant seedlings is at the onset of the wet season. Nursery activities must be timed so the seedlings are in optimal condition and ready for the field at the proper time to be outplanted.

As mentioned in the section about containers, growing tree seedlings is predominantly about the root system. A healthy, actively growing root system with good form is key to outplanting success. Timing is essential in this aspect, because regardless of the type of container, seedlings can become rootbound. A tree becomes rootbound when its growth begins to decline because of the limited amount of space available for root development. Root activity continues to decrease until the plant becomes progressively less and less able to regenerate roots and grow. Once its growth has been restricted, a tree will never be able to catch up to other koa seedlings that have not been restricted in their growth. In fact, there are a number of cases when planters have paid a lot of money for larger specimen koa trees in larger pots, only to discover within a few months or years that the trees' growth is far outpaced by a small but vigorous seedling planted nearby at the proper time. It does not take long for a koa tree to reach a rootbound stage. For this reason, koa seedlings must be outplanted promptly when they are ready.

Seedlings are ready when their stems are strong, they have good but not excessive height, their roots are well-developed enough to come out of the container intact, and they have plenty of growth momentum.

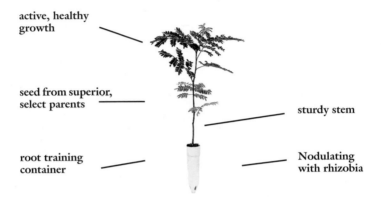

active, healthy growth

seed from superior, select parents

root training container

sturdy stem

Nodulating with rhizobia

Characteristics of a high quality koa seedling

Chapter 6: Preparation

Once the idea to plant koa trees has formed, there is often a strong urge to "get planting!" However, it should be noted that the moment of actually planting the tree in the ground is just a small part of the time and investment required for successful tree planting. In most cases, tree planting is preceded by what often is the most expensive and time consuming aspect of tree planting: site preparation. In order for the planted tree to thrive, the area where the tree will be planted must be well prepared in advance.

Animals including horses, cows, sheep and goats eat koa with relish—and should be excluded before planting

Protecting the Area

Fencing

Koa seedlings are attractive food to grazing and browsing animals including cattle, horses, sheep, deer, and goats. In fact, in other parts of the tropics the foliage of koa relatives in the *Acacia* family are used as a nutritious and palatable animal feed, much as alfalfa is used in temperate areas. Cattle will seek out and eat koa foliage in preference to grass.

The other side of the fence—Where livestock are excluded (right) koa trees can thrive

It has happened many times that a koa planting has been eaten with relish by a neighbor's stray cow or horse. Pigs are also known to bite off koa seedlings, although more commonly they destroy seedlings not by eating them directly but by uprooting the seedlings to get to the worms in the moist soil underneath.

If cattle, sheep, horses, goats, or pigs are present near the area where koa trees will be planted, they should be excluded with fencing. If necessary, any remaining populations within the protected area should be removed.

Fencing will also protect the trees as they grow, since livestock damage adolescent trees by stripping off bark (or in the case of pigs, sharpening their tusks on it), browsing any foliage in reach, and trampling the sensitive root systems. As a native Hawaiian tree, koa did not co-evolve with any large animals, and therefore has no protection, such as thorns or bad odors, against them. Koa root systems also have a very thin outer layer that is easily damaged by trampling.

Left: Some pigs like to use small koa as chew toys; *Left Center*: Freshly stripped bark, a tasty snack for horses; *Right Center*: Wounds from bark damage often heal badly, and compromise the health of the tree; *Right*: A long strip of bark likely torn off by pigs or goats

Other Protection

Other threats to recently planted koa trees include humans, wind, frost (at high elevations), pests, diseases, and weeds.

It takes more that a sign to keep the pigs out

Seedlings can be damaged or destroyed by human traffic including pedestrians, bicycles, joggers, etc. In addition, maintenance activities around the koa trees themselves or the surrounding landscape, such as weedeating, mowing, or herbicide spraying, can kill the seedlings. For example, koa is extremely intolerant of herbicide drift, and will sometimes die if only a few drops of herbicide touch their leaves. In most cases simply marking the trees well and performing careful maintenance around them can preclude damage. However, tree planters should analyze if other protection will be necessary in their case, especially if trees were planted near areas with a lot of human activity.

Wind may also be an issue on some sites. Koa trees can tolerate some wind. However, they do not thrive when exposed to windy conditions. Wind is a constant stress to a koa tree. It can strip moisture from the leaves and tear off foliage. Wind can cause young trees to break, flag (lean over), and/or develop a crooked, branching form. In areas where the goal of planting is ecological rather than economic, this may not be a major concern. If good form and faster growth is desired, however, areas with wind may require a windbreak planted several years in advance of planting the koa. Individual windscreens can be used when planting trees for landscaping, but these are not always effective when the wind comes from variable directions.

On windy sites unprotected koa seedlings will be stressed and poorly formed

Koa grows up to over 7,000 feet (2,134 m) elevation, into areas that receive frost. Frost can kill young seedlings. In high elevations, aside from planting young seedlings in the warmest time of the year, people working in such conditions have reported two effective measures to counter frost: at Keauhou Ranch in Volcano, planting near other trees that are over six feet (1.8 m) tall helps to moderate the temperature (Scowcroft p. comm). In the Hakalau National Wildlife Refuge, small screens of dense shade cloth are used to encourage koa seedlings to open their stomata later in the day when there is warmth, rather than at first light when the trees may take in icy air (Horiuchi p. comm.)

Temporary frost screens can greatly increase survival in open areas at higher elevations (pictured: Cynthia Thurkins)

Pests and diseases may also be a threat to the survival of koa seedlings. However, these are not usually actively managed. Using the best and most site-suitable genetic material, inoculating with rhizobia and mycorrhizae, maintaining diversity by interplanting the koa with other species, planting at the right time of year to minimize stress on the seedlings, and managing attentively are all hoped to aid in mitigating the risks of pests and diseases.

Weeds are also a hazard to the survival of young koa seedlings. Rapidly growing grasses and shrubby weeds can out-compete koa seedlings quickly, causing the young trees to succumb to water or light deprivation. Vines

such as banana poka (*Passiflora mollissima*), German ivy (*Senecio mikanioides*), and hitch-hiker (*Desmodium spp.*) can smother seedlings. Weeds should be well under control before any seedlings are planted, and ongoing strategies for managing weeds planned in advance, as discussed in the next section.

Weedy vines can quickly cover a koa tree. *Left*: Banana poka; *Right*: Honeysuckle and banana poka double-whammy

Preparing the Planting Site

Land preparation can make all the difference between a successful and unsuccessful project. Regardless of the type of preparation to be done, the schedule for it should be planned in advance so it is timed to be completed before the koa seedlings from the nursery are ready, but not too early. Nature doesn't like a vacuum; clearing vegetation and then waiting several months (or worse, years) is a guarantee that invasive weeds will move in, and the preparation work will have to be repeated. Land preparation should ideally be scheduled to be complete about four weeks in advance of the planting date.

The kind of preparation depends on the type of planting site. These can be divided into roughly five types:

Herbaceous Grassy lawns and yards, pastures, or sugarcane fields

Exotic woody Usually former pasture or cleared areas, these fields are covered in thickets of exotic woody vegetation. These can include Christmas berry, strawberry guava, albizias, and ironwood.

Mixed forest/open native forest Native forest (usually ʻōhiʻa lehua) with either open areas due to grazing or development damage, or pockets of invasive species that will be removed

Farms Orchard or cropland

Lava field Not recommended for koa

It is beyond the scope of this book to discuss land preparation strategies in detail. Appropriate land preparation should be developed in cooperation with a land use planner. For areas over one acre (0.4 hectare) where soil disturbance is considered, a Conservation Plan and historical survey can be developed with the Natural Resource Conservation Service (NRCS) and the local Soil and Water Conservation District (SWCD).

In general, some of the strategies used on these types of sites are as follows:

Herbaceous

Young koa trees to not do well in competition with grass, and should never be planted directly into grass. Grass should be removed from the planting site, or at a minimum from an area at least four feet (1.2 m) in diameter where the tree will be planted (and well maintained thereafter).

For individual trees planted as landscaping, grass is often controlled by hand scalping, mowing or weedeating the area to be planted close to the ground. If the grass resprouts, it can be sprayed with herbicide. Two applications (two to four weeks apart) are sometimes necessary to ensure the grass has died.

Some projects planting into grassy pasture use a small machine such as a D-4 with a small blade mounted on it to scrape off the grass surface at each planting spot, clearing an area about four feet (1.2 m) square. The tree is then planted in the center of the square.

Open and degraded pasture, Hamakua, Hawaiʻi

After the initial preparation, grass can be kept down with a good mulch and/or groundcover and hand-weeding maintenance, and/or with continued herbicide applications as necessary. As the trees grow, they will eventually form a shady canopy that will reduce the need for grass control after a year or more.

Sugarcane, while technically a grass, is very competitive and planters may consider some of the strategies used for woody vegetation.

Exotic Woody Vegetation

Sites that are covered with thickets of exotic species such as Christmas berry, strawberry guava, or sugarcane are challenging. Often the heavy vegetation is removed with the help of some kind of machinery. Commonly used methods are:

- sawing trees and chipping/mulching (sometimes combined with chemical control to prevent resprouting)
- shredding with a brushhog (for sugarcane or small brush, again often followed by herbicide to kill resprouts)
- bulldozing (with cleared brush pushed into mounds along the contour for erosion control and to keep the organic matter on the site), or
- careful clearing with an excavator.

The manager must determine the kind of clearing appropriate to the site.

Thick growth of species such as strawberry guava can be challenging to remove

Remnant ʻōhiʻa in former pasture, North Kona

It is important to inventory the site carefully before considering heavy machinery. While it is commonly the case that these kinds of thickets form on land that was once completely cleared (usually for pasture or sugarcane), sometimes landholders are delighted to find pockets of native vegetation or even structures such as rock walls and terraces. Clearing with a chainsaw or by hand is a slow and laborious process, but can save important plants and land features. And always in Hawaiʻi, a conservation plan by the NRCS and SWCD and a survey for important archeological sites is advised (and often required) prior to using any heavy machinery.

Mixed Forest

Planting into existing forest is called "enrichment planting" or "gap planting." Because it often takes place in native areas, care should be taken to create a minimum of site disturbance. If the planting site is open forest with grass patches, low-impact use of strategies mentioned for lawns and pastures, done in patches, is effective. Where the use of chemical herbicides is undesirable, cutting back grass manually and then using a weed barrier such as cardboard, mulch, or purchased weed barrier (let sit for 4–12 weeks for grass to die underneath) can be used.

If woody exotics have invaded, careful clearing of these by hand (with a chainsaw) or with small machinery (such as a carefully operated excavator) can be done.

Farm

Farms may consist of one or several of the types of vegetation listed above, and should be prepared accordingly. In addition, placement and planning will be necessary to protect both crops and the koa. Human traffic and activities damage koa's sensitive surface root systems. On the other hand, koa's fast-growing surface roots can also cause future difficulties by aggressive growth, disrupting water lines or competing with crops.

Plantations can be diversified by boundary plantings of koa

Lava

It is not recommended to plant koa into lava. However, some people do it anyway. Rather than involve expensive machinery and impose a planting grid on the land, it is often more successful to imitate the process of natural regeneration on lava. This is achieved by searching out the most hospitable microclimates on the site, the pockets where organic matter and moisture accumulate and other vegetation is beginning to emerge. These are usually fissures in the lava where the trees can get their roots down. Aʻa flows are usually much more successfully planted than pahoehoe.

Aʻa lava flow in South Kona

Special Site Preparation

Hawaiʻi is a mosaic of remarkably diverse soils and climates. Some sites hold special challenges. For example, some projects must consider if ripping or hoe ramming will help, if there is soil compaction, pahoehoe lava, or hard pan. It can also be effective to only plant in spots where trees can get their roots deeper into the ground.

Special machinery may be required for compacted agricultural lands

Marking the Planting Spots

After the planting site has been prepared and competing vegetation has been controlled, it is time to prepare the planting holes. The first step is to mark out the individual planting spots according to the spacing and layout determined in the planning phase. The planting spots can be marked out with stakes (bamboo stakes 3–4 feet (0.9–1.2 m) tall with brightly colored surveyor's flagging tied to the top is a good choice).

Surveyor's flagging is a good choice to mark planting spots in a open field (pictured: Kekoa Caverly)

If trees are being planted in rows, each planting spot should still be marked. If a large rock or shallow area is encountered, adjust the location of the planting hole along the row, rather than away from the row. It is more important that each tree get a livable planting spot than that the spacing is perfectly even.

Amending

It is controversial when, if, and how to amend a koa planting site. Most projects choose to amend the planting holes in advance of or on the day of planting. Nitrogen fertilizer should *not* be used. However, amending other nutrients deficient in the soil could aid the koa's growth. Phosphorus, potassium, calcium, or other amendments can be sprinkled evenly in quantities determined by the soil analysis in a small diameter around the planting holes.

Now, it is time to plant!

Chapter 7: Tree Planting

After the planning, nursery work and site preparations are complete, it is at last time to plant the trees! This is a key moment in the tree's life. Poor planting can damage the tree. For example root damage during transplanting may lead to heart rot problems later. Even with careful handling, this can be a stressful time for the tree, so it is crucial that planting be done with care.

It is recommended that a person prepare mentally before planting a tree. The Hawaiian way is to ask permission of the land before entering the area to be planted, and to ask permission of the tree before planting it. As one *Kumu* advised, "Have an intention as you plant each tree, that it grow and thrive."

A well-planted tree (pictured: Kira Gerrits)

Timing

In areas with a pronounced dry season, planting at the onset of the rainy season is usually best (ideally, just after the first few soaking rains). That way the trees can get their roots deeper into the soil and be well established before the dry season. In areas with sufficient rainfall throughout the year, a good time to plant is usually March or April. Koa loves sun and warm weather (as long as the roots get enough water), and the onset of summer is a good time to get them established.

Transporting and Preparing the Seedlings

Once the seedlings are removed from the care and protection of the nursery area, they are subject to new stresses such as wind and lack of water.

Be prepared to plant the trees as soon as possible after removing them from the nursery—ideally within a few hours. If seedlings must be transported, arrange to pick them up when they trees can be planted within 12–48 hours. It will be necessary to water and care for the seedlings if they are not planted in the same day.

During transport from the nursery to the planting site, seedlings must be protected from wind in a closed vehicle. Subjecting seedlings to a ride in the back of a pick-up truck at 55 miles per hour is the same as subjecting them to near hurricane-force winds —and it will likely injure or kill them. Sometimes when subjected to a windy truck ride, the seedlings will look like they survived, only to drop all their leaves and die within a few days. Likewise, seedlings should also not be subjected to temperature extremes. For example, they should never be left in a hot car.

Make sure the seedlings are well-watered just prior to outplanting. A thorough soaking will increase their chances of survival the first few days in the field. As an additional benefit, well-watered seedlings are easier to remove from their containers.

Seedlings must be protected from wind during transport

For transporting the seedlings within the planting site, it is a good idea to keep the trees upright in a bucket or nursery tray to avoid exposing the sides of the containers to direct sun. The heat of the sun can quickly damage or dry out the roots if it hits them directly, severely stressing the tree. Instead, roots should be kept in the potting container and protected from the sun, and quickly transferred from the container to the soil (see next section).

Planting Seedlings

Before planting, the hard work of preparing the land has already been done as described in the previous chapter. Planting trees is a pleasure once land preparation has been done properly. However, tree planting is not a thing to rush. It is important to follow the steps below carefully and focus on one tree at a time. This may mean starting slowly, but once a planter gets the hang of it, efficiency will increase.

1 Make a hole just slightly larger than the size of the root system. For areas where there is good soil, an oʻo bar is a good tool.

2 Remove the seedling from the container. Hold the seedling very lightly by the thickest part of its stem; do not pinch or bruise the stem. If grown to size and well-watered, the root system will slip out easily. Sometimes squeezing the container a little on the sides helps loosen the potting media from the walls so the root system slides out easily. Be patient, never yank or tear the roots.

An oʻo bar can make a hole slightly larger than the container. *Left*: Homemade oʻo bar tip made for plants grown in container on left; *Right*: Commercial planting tool

3 Immediately place the root system in the hole. Remember, koa roots are very sensitive—do not attempt to "fluff them out" or trim them, and do not expose them to full sunlight (if necessary, the person planting can shade the seedling with their torso as they move from the container to the hole).

4 The tree should be planted at the correct depth—the ground even with the root collar (the place where the roots meet the stem—the same level as the container medium).

5 When placing the tree in the planting hole, make sure the root system maintains the form of the container it was grown in (assuming it was a root-training container). Roots should not be squashed into the hole. There are detrimental root conditions called "J–rooting" and "L–rooting" which refer to the shapes of root deformities that can result

Planting may be the most important event in the life of a koa. *Top Left*: Preparing hole slightly larger than the container; *Top Center*: Positioned to plant; *Top Right*: Carefully removing tree from container; *Lower Left*: Planting tree taking care not to damage or bend roots; *Lower Center*: Firming soil around roots; *Lower Right*: Planted and clearly marked with bright flagging (pictured: Kalima Brooks)

from planting incorrectly. The roots should fit easily into the hole so that the root system has good form.

6 Firm the soil around the roots of the tree. This is essential. Soil must contact the roots firmly in order for the tree to survive. Air pockets around the root system could cause the roots to dry and the seedling to die. If possible, this is the time to water the seedling in the ground to "settle" the soil and ensure there are no air pockets. However, if watering is not possible, the soil must be firmed down by hand. After firming the

Plant even with the root collar, the level of the potting medium

soil, check again to make sure the soil is at the correct level (at the root collar).

7 Put in a marking stake (if there is not one already in place from laying out the site). It is important to be able to see where the small seedlings are easily, to avoid damaging them later while walking around or during maintenance. Bamboo stakes 3–4 feet (0.9–1.2 m) tall with a piece of brightly-colored vinyl surveyor's tape tied to the top are recommended. In a recently cleared or maintained area this may seem unnecessary, but after a few weeks the surrounding vegetation can shoot up and make it difficult to

find the seedlings again, causing countless maintenance headaches. It is recommended to leave the flags in the ground until the trees are 5–6 feet (1.5–1.8 m) tall.

Bright marking flags for each tree will protect them during later maintenance

8 On very windy sites, the marking stake may temporarily double as a support for the seedling. Tie loosely, so the tree can flex a little with the wind, using tying materials that will not scar or damage the tree. Remove the tie within a few weeks after the tree is planted. This should only be done if the tree will not stand up straight without being tied.

9 If amendments such as phosphorus will be added, sprinkle uniformly around the seedling, starting a few inches away from the stem.

Young koa fertilized with phosphorous

10 If the soil was not moist enough, it will be necessary to water each seedling slowly and carefully, with about 1–2 gallons of water.

11 Wish the tree well, and move on to the next tree.

Planting Large Koa Seedlings

When planting larger koa trees, the guidelines are similar to the above, with these alterations:

Dig a planting hole as deep as the root ball and about twice its diameter.

For larger containers, especially if soil and not potting media was used, seedlings should be well-watered, but not soggy. Too much water can make the soil heavy and might cause it to fall apart when the tree is removed from its container.

Remove the tree from its container. Poly bags should be cut off. Plastic hard containers should also be cut off if there is any difficulty at all in removing the tree from the container. Use a razor, sharp knife, or sharp clippers. Slit the container carefully, making a cut on either side (only as deep as the plastic, not into the root system itself), then open.

Plant the tree so the ground is even with the root collar (the place where the roots join the stem—the same level of the container media).

If the tree can stay upright in the wind without staking, then it is best not to stake. If the tree is unable to stand up to the wind, the tree can be staked using materials that will not harm the trunk. The staking job should allow some movement so the tree can flex with the wind.

Weed Barrier/Mulch

Many koa plantings take place in rugged conditions with a minimum of time and amenities possible for each tree. However, if koa are being planted where some additional inputs are possible, weed barriers and/or mulch can aid greatly in tree establishment.

Mulch helps with weed suppression and water retention (pictured: Kent Lighter)

Mulching improves nutrient and water retention in the soil, encourages favorable soil microbial activity, and suppresses weed growth. When properly executed, mulching can improve the well-being of plants and reduce maintenance as compared to bare soil culture. A three layered mulch system (sometimes called "sheet mulching" or "lasagna mulching") consisting of worm castings, amendments, and a little compost, a middle layer weed barrier such as cardboard or purchased weed barrier, and a top layer of weed-free organic matter such as leaves, macadamia nut husks, or wood chips can maximize the weed suppression benefits of mulching. Mulch should be about three inches (8 cm) thick, spread in a ring with a radius of 1–3 feet (30–90 cm) from the trunk. Mulch should never touch the stem of the tree, but instead should start 3–6 inches (8–16 cm) away from the trunk. The middle layer of cardboard or other weed barrier is essential, as without it wood chips or other organic matter may cause problems.

Replanting

After a few weeks, there may be some seedling losses. If good care was taken, initial loss is usually less than five or ten percent of the total number of seedlings planted. Losses may be due to stresses in transport, while transplanting, or because of insufficient water after transplanting. Dead seedlings can be pulled out and if desired, the spots can be replanted.

A Few Guidelines to Keep in Mind

DO

- Plan and prepare thoroughly before the planting day.
- Make sure seedlings are well-watered prior to outplanting.
- Plant at the depth where roots spread from the trunk (the collar).
- Keep the seedlings watered at least to the depth of the roots.
- Mark the tree with a stake and bright flagging
- Create an intention that the tree lives and thrives.

DO NOT

- Do not allow seedlings to dry out.
- Do not prune, trim, or otherwise "fluff out" the koa seedling roots.
- Do not tear, shake, or wash out the potting media from the root system.
- Do not plant too shallow or to deep.
- Do not prune or trim branches at planting time.
- Do not brace or stake unless the tree cannot stand without it.
- Do not allow grass near the tree's root zone.
- Do not spray herbicide in a way that any drift or drops will touch the tree.

Chapter 8: Management

Maintenance and management of young koa seedlings is usually most intensive in the first 3–12 months after planting. The focus during early maintenance is to help the koa trees get above the surrounding vegetation. This requires keeping the koa seedlings free from competitive weeds and grass, which enables them to receive full sunlight, have access to water and soil nutrients, and get established quickly. In dry areas, supplemental water may be necessary to ensure survival, and can also boost early growth. Other management activities may include ongoing animal control, fertilization, weed management, and thinning.

Weed control is an essential part of establishing seedlings (pictured: Mark Kimball, Carlos Valdovinos and Kim Wilkinson discussing Mark's strategy)

Watering

Seedlings should not be allowed to dry out during establishment. In dry conditions, daily watering for the first week or two will help the seedling's establishment, followed by water every three to seven days for the next three months. In very dry areas, occasional waterings might be necessary for up to a year.

Early monitoring and management will help seedlings survive (pictured: author Kim Wilkinson)

Each watering should be thorough and deep, done by hand with a gentle flow of water, or by drip irrigation emitters. Deep waterings encourage tree roots to grow deeper in the soil, which will make it easier for them to "fend for themselves" later in acquiring water and surviving drought periods. In contrast, shallow waterings (such as often achieved with overhead sprinklers) encourage the tree's roots to grow very close to the surface. In such cases, when the irrigation water is cut off, the shallow root system is not shaped to forage deep in the soil. During droughts, the soil surface is the first to dry out.

Weed Control

Weed and grass control is extremely important during the early months and years to reduce competition and to improve seedling survival and growth. As a shade-intolerant species, koa can be stunted or even killed if surrounding vegetation reduces its access to full sunlight.

Some of the ways people manage weeds around koa is through hand weeding, ground covers, and mulch; herbicide applications; or by mechanical means (weedeating and mowing). Close to the seedlings, any emerging weeds are hand pulled or very carefully touched with herbicide. Koa is extremely sensitive to herbicide, and care must be taken that no herbicide drops or mist touch the young trees. Hand weeding usually takes place between two and four times during the first year, and one or two times a year thereafter.

Once the koa trees are of good height (usually after one to four years), their canopies shade the understory enough to suppress some of the most aggressive weeds. Thereafter, ongoing maintenance such as hand weeding, weed cutting, or herbicide application will occasionally be necessary.

Eliminating competitive weeds from the root zone can be achieved with mulch and hand weeding

Fertilization

There may be an initial amending of the soil during or prior to planting, to adjust pH and supplement nutrient deficiencies such as phosphorus and calcium. Amendments are usually sprinkled on the soil surface around the planting hole. If the soil is very poor, subsequent applications of amendments, especially phosphorus, during the first few years may boost koa growth. Since koa are nitrogen-fixing, no nitrogen fertilizer should be applied.

Pruning

Koa trees should not be pruned if it can be avoided. Pruning slows their growth and greatly increases their susceptibility to diseases and pests. In many cases, good planning, superior genetics, and close spacing are enough to preclude the need for pruning most trees. In the best scenarios, most of the lower branches die and fall off of their own accord (called "self-pruning").

Pruning koa often does more harm than good; this pruning wound did not heal, and the heartwood is rotting with no hope of recovery

In some cases, however, problematic tree form such as forks or excessive lateral branching may develop, and the manager must decide if the benefits of pruning outweigh the risks. If so, pruning should still be absolutely minimal, using proper pruning techniques that minimize damage and facil-itate healing of the wound.

To prune or not to prune? Pruning should be avoided wherever possible. If it must be done, it should be minimal, done properly, without excessive injury to the tree

Thinning

When koa is grown in dense stands, close initial spacing is often used to facilitate straight tree form. However, koa trees grow fast and quickly begin to compete with each other, slowing or even stagnating each other's growth. If close spacing is used, thinning will be required after a few years. As with many other aspects of koa management, there is no set recommendation of exactly when and how this is best done—although ongoing research might produce some more specifics soon. In general, most projects mark out the "keepers"—the fastest growing trees with the best form—and proceed to remove surrounding trees as needed as they begin to touch the canopy of the best trees. This process is called "releasing," since the best trees are released from competition from their immediate neighbors. Thinning usually takes place two to three times during the first 3–15 years to release the trees with the best form and vigor. After thinning, the trees that remain will have more space and better access to light, nutrients and water.

The optimal final density of a koa planting is also unknown. Some projects have final densities as high as over 100 koa trees per acre (250/hectare), others less than half that, and still others with less than a handful of koa trees per acre. Any project considering

commercial returns must consider thinning and final tree density carefully, ideally in consultation with a forester and/or extension specialist.

Overcrowding threatens koa's survival, health, and growth. Early thinning allows the best trees to grow and thrive.

Pests, Diseases, and Other Damaging Agents

(contributions by Brian Bushe)

The incompatibility of livestock and koa has been emphasized repeatedly. In areas where there is risk of damage by livestock, ongoing maintenance and animal control is required. This includes periodically checking fence lines to make sure they are effectively excluding animals, and if necessary catching or hunting within the planting area for animals such as pigs and goats.

There are many pests and diseases that affect koa. Koa is susceptible to both native and introduced pests and diseases. In a landscape setting, some of these are managed (see Heidi Bornhorst, page 70), but for most koa plantings, they are often not managed. Using a local site-adapted seed source, maintaining overall good health of the trees (by avoiding pruning and root disturbances) and interplanting koa with a diversity of other species are thought to help minimize the risks. On some sites, such as lowland areas particularly susceptible to *Fusarium* or twig-borers, a significant percentage of losses is to be expected.

Some of the most serious pests and diseases of of koa include the following (Friday 2000 and Gardner 1996):

- *Fusarium* spp.: Usually *Fusarium oxysporum*, fungus that causes a wilt disease and leads to decline or death of koa trees.
- *Calonectria* spp: including *Calonectria crotalariae* (causes crown rot) and *Calonectria theae* (causes a shoot blight).
- Scolytid beetles: *Xylosandrus compactus* (black twig borer) and *Xyleborus* sp.

- The koa moth (*Scotorythra paludicola*) can completely defoliate entire koa stands, slowing growth and sometimes leading to the death of 30% or more of the trees in the stand.

Rust Fungi

Rust fungi (order *Uredinales*) are some of the most easily spotted and widespread diseases of koa. Five different species of rust fungi associated with koa in Hawai'i. Identification is best achieved by comparing host symptoms. Some produce deformities of leaves, shoots, branches or stems referred to as "witches' broom."

Above left: Wilt possibly caused by the fungi *Fusarium oxysporum* f. sp. *koae*; *Above center:* Trunk exhibiting symptom of a fungal canker; *Above right:* 'Bleeding' caused by scolytid beetle infestation (possibly black twig borer *Xylosandrus compactus*) (photos: Jay Hatayama)

Twig borers can cause major damage or mortality at lower elevations. *Left:* Typical twig borer damage evidenced by dying branch tip; *Right:* Twig borer gallery showing borer and associated ambrosia fungus

Above left: Typical rust pustule on phyllodes; *Above right:* 'Witches' broom' symptom associated with systemic infection of certain species of rust fungi

Left: Sooty mold on true leaves of young tree; *Right:* Sooty mold on phyllodes of mature tree

- *Atelocauda koae*—produces no brooms
- *Atelocauda digitata*—produces brooms about 6 inches (15 cm) tall
- *Atelocauda agustiphylloda*—produces very large brooms up to 3 feet (0.9 m) tall
- *Endoraecium acaciae*—Produces conspicuous, profusely branched brooms
- *Endoraecium hawaiiensis*—found on Oʻahu

Sooty mold

Sooty molds (composed of many different fungi) often develop on plants as a superficial, black growth of fungal mycelium. These fungi are not parasitic but live off the "honey dew" which is the sugary excrement of certain Homopteran insects (ie. aphids, whiteflies, mealybugs, etc.). The acacia psyllid (*Psylla uncatoides*) is a homopteran insect that is a common pest of koa and produces much honey dew. The sooty molds restrict koa growth by covering the leaves.

Miscellaneous pests. *Above left:* Spiraling whitefly (showing waxy lines, forming a somewhat spiraling pattern); *Above center:* Beetle feeding damage, perhaps Fuller rose beetle, *Asynonychus godmani*, an occasional seasonal problem at higher elevations; *Above right:* No insects present—symptoms resemble mite/thrips feeding damage

 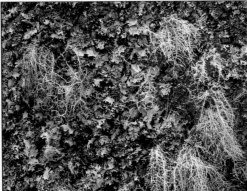

Long Live Lichens! Lichens are a stabilized thallus of two plants, an alga and a fungus, and are therefore not pathogens. *Left:* Crustose lichen on young tree; *Right:* Fruticose lichen on mature tree

Beyond Koa

A forest is more than the trees. Trees are connected with many other organisms in ways that ensure long-term survival for the trees and their forest community. Extinctions, environmental changes, competitive and invasive species, and other challenges mean that native ecosystems that have been degraded cannot be returned to their original condition. Conservation of remaining native Hawaiian forests and ecosystems is vital.

However, by planting koa in landscapes, degraded pastures, or agricultural lands, can we hope to regenerate any other aspects of koa forests as well?

Climate

Trees do affect the climate. Growing trees can reduce surrounding air temperatures, provide shade, improve watersheds, conserve moisture, remove dust and pollutants from the air, and even accumulate fog drip from the air. People planting koa in drought-plagued areas that once enjoyed regular rainfall are trusting in the wisdom of the Hawaiian proverb: "Rains always follow the forest."

Many planters wonder if planting koa with agri-culture can create wildlife habitat or other benefits

Birds

Many endangered Hawaiian birds today depend on koa for nesting, habitat, and as a source for insect food sources. People who plant koa often wonder if they can hope to attract native birds to their koa trees.

However, most native Hawaiian birds are kept out of agricultural and residential areas by more than just lack of food source and habitat. Native Hawaiian birds need large areas of contiguous habitat and dense forest that includes older koa trees. Most won't cross open areas. Predators, exotic competitors, and introduced diseases including avian malaria are big threats to bird populations. Where these threats remain, native Hawaiian birds cannot expand into reforested areas. At present, the challenges of restoring some native Hawaiian bird habitat across landscapes may seem insurmountable. However, some researchers are hopeful that one day there could be a remedy or preven-tative measures for avian malaria, and this and other protections may enable some native Hawaiian birds to once again expand their range.

In the meantime, the best hope for protecting Hawai'i's native birds from further extinctions is to conserve large areas of forests and support the protection and management of these areas in parks, conservation areas, and private landholdings. Supporting restoration efforts will also lead to more information about how to not only conserve but expand habitat. For example, in the Hakalau National Wildlife Refuge where koa is being replanted in former pasture, a few native birds have begun to be seen among the planted koa trees (Horiuchi, p. comm.). This is a promising beginning.

Native Hawaiian Plants

Planting some of koa's associated plant species can certainly be successful. The high litter production and nitrogen fixing capability of koa provide fertility and water-conserving mulch to the plants around it. Koa is generous in supporting the other plants and trees in its domain (as long as the koa gets to be in the canopy!).

Why not diversify koa's community by planting some other native or Polynesian plants? In natural forests, there are more than 80 plant species are known to be associated with koa. Understory plants and other trees can thrive around koa.

Plants to consider depend on the environment of the planting site. It is recommended to do some reading about what sorts of native plants grow well in the area to be planted, as Hawai'i's ecosystems are amazingly diverse.

A few examples include:

Trees and shrubs:

'ōhi'a lehua (*Metrosideros polymorpha*): the most abundant native tree, a widespread forest companion of koa

wiliwili (*Erythrina sandwicensis*): Hawaiian coral tree

loulu (*Pritchardia* spp.): native palms

alahe'e (*Canthium odoratum*): a coffee/gardenia relative with fragrant flowers

māmaki (*Pipturis albidus*): edible/medicinal uses for people, also provides food for native butterflies

naio (*Mycoporum sandwicense*): has a fragrant and scented wood

'a'ali'i (*Dodonaea viscosa*): a tough and widely-adapted native shrub

koki'o ke'oke'o (*Hibiscus* spp.): Hawaiian white hibiscus

mamane (*Sophora chrysophylla*): a tree (sometimes shrub) with medicial uses

kauila (*Alphitonia ponderosa*): A tree with hard, heavy, dark red wood that sinks in water

hapu'u (*Cibotium glaucum*): Hawaiian tree fern

Vines, fillers, and groundcovers:

maile (*Alyxia oliviformis*): a favorite lei material, very fragrant

'ilima papa (*Sida fallax*): a low groundcover with yellow flowers

'ūlei (*Osteomeles anthyllidifolia*): white, fragrant flowers and glossy green leaves

'ākia (*Wikstroemia uva-ursi*): a drought-tolerant groundcover

kupukupu, 'okupukupu (*Nephrolepis cordi-flolia*): a native sword fern

palapalai (*Microlepia stringosa*): a.k.a. "palai," a fern, favorite of lei makers.

Also, certain areas deemed unsuitable for koa planting might also consider planting koa's close relative, koai'a (*Acacia koaia*), a more lowland and drought-resistant species. It has a smaller form, and the wood is highly valued.

Above left: 'A'ali'i, a common forest companion of koa; *Above Right:* Naio

Left: Famous flower of 'ōhi'a lehua; *Center:* New flush of 'ōhi'a lehua; *Right:* Hapu'u fern

Chapter 9: Perspectives

Nainoa Thompson

Navigator, Polynesian Voyaging Society, Hawai'i

When our ancestors built and sailed voyaging canoes, it required the labor and arts of the entire community, everyone working together—some collecting the materials in the forest, others weaving the sails, carving the hulls, lashing, preparing food for the voyage, or performing rituals to protect the crew at sea. So we thought that building a canoe of traditional materials would bring our entire community together, not just the sailors, but the crafts people, artists, chanters, dancers and carvers. The Native Hawaiian Culture and Arts Program was set up to build not just a canoe—but a sense of community—by recreating Hawaiian culture.

Departure ceremony of Hokule'a voyage to Rapa Nui, Hilo, Hawai'i, June 1999 (photo: © Monte Costa)

We started in our koa forests and ended up finding that in the last 80–100 years, ninety percent of our koa trees have been cut down. The ecosystem that once supported this healthy forest is in trouble. We could not find a single koa tree that was big enough and healthy enough to build one hull of a canoe.

On our last weekend of the search, in the Kilauea Forest Reserve on the island of Hawai'i, we searched with a large team and found nothing. Everyone went back to work on Monday, but Tava Taupu and I stayed in the forest. We decided that Tuesday, March 18, was our last day. At that point I was very project oriented—we have a job, we've got to build a canoe—but inside I was sad and depressed by the difference between what I imagined our native forests to look like and what they actually looked like. All around us were alien species and ferns uprooted by feral pigs introduced to Hawai'i in the 19th century. I saw a layer of banana poka vines twisting in the canopy from one tree to another, choking the trees.

"There's a fence-line up ahead about a half mile," I told Tava. "I'll go up slope and we'll work toward it together to cover more ground. We'll meet at the fence. If we don't find anything, that will be it."

Tava nodded and began moving forward. We knew that we were not going to find any trees, that the search was going to fail, but it was our last chance. When I saw Tava and he saw me, from that moment, we never spoke. We each knew the other had not found a tree. We did not even walk on the same side of the road. Tava walked behind me, as if we were repelled by each other. We were very depressed. We had not achieved what we so much wanted to achieve. But beyond that, I think the loss of the forest was eroding something inside of us.

There was another source of trees for Hawaiian canoes. We knew trees from the Pacific Northwest drifted to Hawai'i, and our ancestors cherished them and built canoes from them. Herb Kane and I had talked about our project earlier with his old friend, Tlingit elder Judson Brown, who was chairman of the board of Sealaska, a native Alaskan timber corporation. Judson fully understood what we were trying to do. It was about reviving our culture, and he knew the trees were the tools for doing that. Without hesitation, he said, "We will give you trees for your canoe if you need them."

Nainoa Thompson (photo: © Monte Costa, courtesy Polynesian Voyaging Society)

After we ended our search for koa trees, we called on Judson and Sealaska and gave them the specifications for the two trees we needed. They said they would search, and they did for six weeks in the remotest parts of their forests in Alaska. Then they called us up and said, "We have the trees of your specifications. But we're not going to cut them down unless you come up here and tell us it's okay. Because we believe that our people are connected to the natural environment, that the trees and the forests are family to our people. And we're not going to take the life of a family member unless we know this is what you want."

I was in charge of building a canoe. That was my narrow focus. But around this project were so many layers of values that I did not clearly see. I understood them, I felt them, but I did not see them as part of my responsibilities. I was thinking of deadlines and logistics. Judson gave me a new perspective based on the values of his elders; it's the kind of wisdom that we always seek from the older generation.

So we flew up to Alaska. We got a helicopter in Ketchikan and went west 80 miles to a remote forest on Shelikof Island. Our guide was Ernie Hillman, a forest manager for Sealaska. He had done his job. The trees were exactly what we asked for. But when he asked me, "Shall we cut these trees down?" I couldn't answer him. I didn't want to cut the trees down. They were too beautiful, too full of life. I began to weigh the value of our project against the value of the life of the trees. I was just too troubled. Everybody got real quiet. I couldn't explain myself. The trees were breath-taking—I had never seen trees like that before, giant evergreens. I began to sense Alaska's power. There was something so very different about it, something alluring. It was very spiritual, and that made me quiet and humble. The place was so wild, so clean and still, so natural. I began to face up to the reckless changes taking place in Hawai'i, especially on O'ahu. When I was a kid I felt very lucky to be from here—and I still do—but the reefs in Maunalua Bay were still alive back then, and now they are dead. We got back on the helicopter, and no one talked. We flew back to Honolulu. The trees remained in the forest.

Something was wrong. I didn't know what it was. I talked to Auntie Agnes Cope and John Dominis Holt, our elders who were on the Board of the Native Hawaiian Culture and Arts Program which was supporting this project to build a canoe called Hawai'iloa. Why didn't I ask for the trees to be cut down? It was because by taking the trees out of Alaska, we were walking away from the pain and the destruction of our native Hawaiian forests. We could not take the life of a tree from another place unless we dealt with the environmental abuse in our own homeland. The answer was clear. Our elders told me, "You know what the answers are. To deal with the abuse here, you need to do something to renew our forests. Before you cut down somebody else's trees, you need to plant your own." So we started a program at Kamehameha Schools to plant koa trees; and we've planted over 11,000 koa seedlings, in hopes that in 100 years, we might have forests of trees for voyaging canoes.

At the planting, I remember grandchildren with grandparents, a big circle of people participating in healing the forest. It was a diverse group. There was a growing sense of community. What started as a project of artisans and people within the Hawaiian voyaging community now extended out as far away as Alaska.

This event brought closure to the search for koa trees by recognizing that we had a real problem in our land. Even though the planting was symbolic, we were contributing in a way that was sending the right kind of message to our communities about replacing abuse with renewal. This became a fundamental value which began to permeate all our decisions. It was the groundwork for what guides us today—Malama Hawai'i, taking care of Hawai'i, our special island home.

(This perspective was adapted from Thompson 2000.)

Benton Keali'i Pang

Botanist, U.S. Fish and Wildlife Service, Pacific Islands Ecoregion

I'll discuss canoe making as it was practiced in ancient times and how it's been applied today by the Polynesian Voyaging Society. I will also discuss some of the rights and responsibilities that we feel Hawaiian organizations and non-Hawaiian organizations can help out in preserving our koa forests, as well as where we as a community in Hawai'i can go from here.

The koa forests were an extremely important resource for Hawaiians. There is a dichotomy between where the Hawaiians lived, called the *wao kanaka,* and the *wao akua,* those forested areas which were important to the gods. The chiefs, who were walking representations of the gods, were not owners of the resources nor owners of the land. They were more stewards or trustees of these resources. So, in these *wao akua,* these dominions of the gods, strict protocol has to be followed in order to enter them for gathering koa, medicinal plants, house-construction plants, bird catching, and the like.

There was strict *kapu* here. One of the values practiced in ancient times was that of *kapu* prohibition. And there were also places that were free, *noa.* These were the habitation areas where Hawaiians could freely walk and converse with one another and sometimes even gather plants. There was also the *'ai kapu,* which prohibited men and women from eating with one another. So there was prohibition, but there also were places that were considered *noa,* or free. There were also the values of *'ike,* knowledge, and that of *malama,* or stewardship that in order to know what to gather, you have to know sometimes the life cycle, you have to know the qualities of, say, the wood, if you are gathering for weapons, or for canoes. Also, you had to know that after you gather the resource, what are you going to do give back, the *malama,* the stewardship responsibilities. Are you going to clear around that patch of *olona* and enhance it, make it larger, or are you going to use some other aspect of conservation which would make sure the resource is there when you or your family member goes back to collect those resources.

In the *ahupua'a,* there was this balance of *lokahi.* There were terrestrial resources and there were ocean resources, and they all belonged to the *ahupua'a.* So ocean-land balance is very important to Hawaiians, and this comes to them from genealogical chants. The spirituality of Hawaiians is talked about in the genealogical chants, where the Hawaiians were born from, the different species both marine and terrestrial which had counterparts with one another. For every land species there was an ocean counterpart, and after the evolution of these species came the Hawaiian people. So Hawaiians, in the religious aspect, looking at natural resources in the land in the ocean, were actually born from it. The resources were actually a part of them, sometimes regarded as our *kupuna,* our ancestors, sometimes regarded as our *'aumakua,* or spirits.

Like all aspects of Hawaiian culture, the gathering of koa for canoe-making was a religious undertaking. The specialist here was a guild of woodcutters or wood craftsmen called *kahuna kalai wa'a,* those men who carved the canoe, or the *wa'a.* Once a tree was found in the forest by one of these *kahuna kalai wa'a,* he would come down from the forest to tell other men that there's a tree that they could possibly use for making a canoe. All the men would sleep in the *hale mua,* the men's house, and would make certain prayers and offerings to the gods. The next day they would proceed up into the forest. The number of these men were many, because you needed men to sharpen the adze heads as the tree was being cut, you needed men to lash the adzes as they were being cut because it would take quite a long time, and then you[1] needed special carvers to know how to precisely carve out this large koa tree into a dugout canoe.

Before entering the forest, chants were given by the *kahuna kalai wa'a.* Once permission was granted from *Ku* of the forest, which was the god of this forest region, they would come to the base of the koa tree and again they would sleep together and make specific offerings of red fish, pig, and coconut, and the next day, the third day, they would proceed to cut the tree. Once the tree was felled, they would wait for a sign, and the sign is that of the *'elepaio* bird. Those of you who are zoologists know that the *'elepaio* bird is a very territorial bird and, we say locally, *niele,* it likes to see what's going on in its territory. So, the Hawaiians saw this as a sign that the bird is checking the koa tree to make sure it's fit to be

cut into a canoe. The *'elepaio* bird would come to fly on top of this felled koa tree and peck at it or not peck at it. If it pecked, the *kahuna kalai wa'a* would know that the log was infested with insects, and the men would then return back to their houses and wait for another day to cut down a tree. If the *'elepaio* bird did not peck at the tree, then the partial hewing of the log would continue.

Now this *'elepaio* bird was also seen as a sign of Lea. Lea is the wife of Ku. Remember Ku is the god of the forest, so the dualism here is his wife, Lea, also has an important aspect in the making of the canoe tree. And this is kind of important in that there is so much dependency on a female goddess for this particular activity. You don't find this very often in other aspects of Hawaiian culture and especially in resource gathering.

The canoe was almost completely made up in the forest. After felling the tree, the branches were cut off, it was debarked, and it was shaped. To get it down to the canoe shed, which always was located near the coast, it took a large group of people and this would now include women and sometimes even children to help pull and push the log from the upper forest (and sometimes this could be more than 3,000–4,000 feet in elevation) down to the coast. They would use the cordage from the *hau* tree or sometimes *'akia,* which are very fibrous plants, and lash it onto the canoe, and there would actually be a type of steersmen guiding the log down the hill or down the mountain, making sure it didn't hit any large rocks or trees. It was actually a sort of fun affair. I think it would be very similar to the stamping party of making a *lo'i,* if you're familiar with that, so a large group of people would come out and help.

Then the canoe would be further fashioned at the canoe house. The other parts of the canoe would be put on: the gunnels, the seats, the decking, the mast, if need be. So, the koa was always looked at as an important resource and even into the ocean when it took its first float, the *kahuna kalai wa'a* would give his blessing and then the canoe would then be lifted of the *kapu* and would hopefully be free to make either safe journey for inter-island or safe journey for fishing.

That's one aspect of use of the koa tree in ancient Hawaiian culture, and it's been tried to be applied today by the Polynesian Voyaging Society with the making of the Hawai'iloa; however, the *kahuna kalai wa'a* could not find large enough koa trees in our Hawaiian forests because, I think, of so much degradation and changes in our forests. They couldn't find large enough koa logs to make the double-hulled canoes that would be good enough for ocean voyaging.

(This perspective was adapted from Pang 1996.)

Candace Lutzow-Felling

Botanist, University of Hawai'i at Manoa

I am studying koa's genetic variation and analyzing the applications for conservation biology and forest management issues for koa forest ecosystems in Hawai'i.

Because so much koa forest has been eradicated, we don't know the full range of adaptability of this tree. We do know that koa is incredibly adaptive, and it's range is much larger than many people think. For example, I've seen koa trees growing as low as 80 feet elevation, growing with pandanus (hala), or with naupaka! I've heard it said that koa will not grow in montane wet forest, but look at the montane areas of Laupahoehoe or Makawao, where heavy fog rolls in each afternoon, and where koa is growing fine. I've even seen koa pioneering on lava flows.

Koa tolerates a broad range of moisture and temperature regimes. When a person is thinking of planting koa trees, they should first consider the type of ecosystem they are in. There are six basic forest ecosystems types: lowland dry, lowland moist, or lowland wet; or montane dry, montane moist, or montane wet. Koa can grow in all of these; however, koa does not tolerate continually wet

rainforest conditions. 'Ohi'a does well in the wet rainforest where there is constant fog, but koa doesn't like that. Koa likes to grow in soils where there is good drainage. Koa also does not tolerate salt spray, which is why it doesn't grow all the way down to the coast.

Candace Lutzow-Felling investigates a pahoehoe lava flow (photo: Pat Felling)

These environmental tolerances are passed on genetically. So if you want to plant koa, you should get seeds from as nearby as you can to grow trees that are well adapted to the site. If you can't get any seeds from nearby, you at least should get seeds from an ecosystem with similar rainfall amounts. Koa is adapted to different rainfall regimes. I think rainfall may actually be even more important than elevation as far as finding seed sources that are adapted to the site. For example, planting in dry leeward areas, a dryland koa seed source will probably do much better than a seed from a wetter windward area at the same elevation. Similarly, wetter windward areas should be planted with trees adapted to those conditions.

Knowing your ecosystem type will also help if you want to interplant koa with other native trees or plants. Of the six ecosystems I mentioned, you can find plants that are also happy in that ecosystem and grow with koa.

Koa can grow in a wide variety of environments, many of which are surprising. *Left:* Coastal, moist habitat at Na Pali Coast, Kaua'i, 350 ft elevation; *Center:* Lowland, moist habitat, Kahana Valley, O'ahu, 600 ft; *Right:* Montane dry habitat, Waimea Canyon, Kaua'i, 3,000 ft (photos: Candace Lutzow-Felling)

For example, in lowland dry areas, native hibiscus, a'ali'i, and naio are good candidates. The *Manual of Flowering Plants of Hawai'i* (Vol.1) has a very good description of ecosystem types and the plants that grow in them.

There is an interesting mystery about koa: how did it get to all the different islands? It can't have traveled on wind currents (the seeds are too heavy); or floated in the ocean (the seeds sink), and it wasn't brought by people because it was here well before the first Polynesians arrived nearly 2,000 years ago. I believe that it must have been birds who spread the seeds. Perhaps birds like the extinct koa finch from Maui, or the greater koa finch or the lesser koa finch that lived on the Big Island. Either these birds or others may well have carried koa seeds to the different islands long ago.

Native birds that feed on koa seeds are extinct now. However, almost every native bird we now have is still dependent on koa in some way, if not directly for food and insect foraging, then for habitat. These include the Maui Parrotbill, 'amakihi, and 'akiapola'au. Koa also serves as a host for many native insects. At least 2,000 species of native insects are specific to or favor koa, such as the Kamehameha Butterfly (*Vanessa tamaeamea*), the Koa bug (*Coleotichus blackburniae*), and the native Blackburn's Butterfly (*Udara blackburni*). Koa even hosts some native land snails.

So without koa, our ecosystems would crash. We need koa!

Heidi Leianuenue Bornhorst

Director, Honolulu Botanical Gardens

Koa in Landscapes

Koa, a large majestic tree of Hawaiian forests, prized by woodworkers and cherished by the people of Hawai'i, can be grown in the landscape. It makes a lovely tree in a large-scale landscape. It thrives at higher elevations (1,500–4,000 feet) in areas of rich soil and medium to high rainfall. It can also be grown at lower elevations and in poorer soil with good horticultural practices and supplemental irrigation.

Some people worry that koa is too large for their garden. I always joked with my dad that if the koa trees I planted in their Makiki yard grew too tall, he could have a new koa surfboard (or koa rocker, or fine calabash) made from the fine high quality wood. For small home gardens, koa's relative koaiʻa (*Acacia koaia*) is a smaller tree from drier locations.

For over 20 years a koa tree has grown in Foster Botanic Garden. We planted it near the ever-popular cannonball and sausage trees. This is not the ideal habitat for koa, but it has been happily growing here, educating countless school children, tourists and other interested visitors at this premiere urban botanical garden.

Heidi Leianuenue Bornhorst with a koa tree in Lanaʻi City (photo: Coleen Carroll)

Liliʻuokalani Botanic Garden, across the freeway from Foster Botanic Garden, has several young koa trees that were planted for Arbor Day and Eagle Scout projects over the last several years. These are growing slowly and doing well.

We planted many koa trees at our Wahiawa Botanical Garden with neighborhood school groups and they do well at this elevation (about 1,000 feet). The best specimens are on a steep slope, with a leguminous groundcover of golden glory (*Arachis pintoi*) (we formerly maintained the slope by rappelling down with a weed eater).

Hoʻomaluhia Koa

Hoʻomaluhia Botanic Garden in Kaneʻohe is a 400-acre botanical garden. It was planned for over 20 years as a cooperative flood control project and city botanical garden (part of the Honolulu Botanical Gardens system). This area gets over 200 inches of rain in some years, and is at a deceptively low elevation, only 200 feet at the highest point, Kilonani mauka.

We collected koa seeds from the lowest possible elevations on Oʻahu. At one point director Paul Weissich had me and fellow horticulturist Dave Miranda searching every corner of Hoʻomaluhia and nearby Kaneʻohe neighborhoods for that "perfect, remnant low elevation forest, a tough durable seed source" for koa.

We field planted hundreds of koa, starting in 1979/80 from half 50-gallon drums. They were to be our canopy tree in the Hawaiian section. We also did tons of scout and volunteer projects planting koa from mostly one-gallon pots.

All was fine for about eight to ten years, until twig borers and fungi descended. The University of Hawaiʻi recommended basal and bark sprays, which we did for a short while. You can spray pesticides like Dursban® or Sevin® as a preventative measure. Some people add a fungicide to the tank mix, but an internal fungus associated with twig borers is hard to control. (Nobody really wants to spray insecticides, fully suited in protective gear, when its 85° outside, even if they agreed to do so in the job interview!)

Sanitation is key. Cut off any dead, diseased, or borer ridden branches and dispose of them in a trash bag or other closed container, (do not compost them!) so the twig borers won't spread and infest other nearby trees. Plan for and maintain healthy soil for koa and other Hawaiian trees. Keeping the trees healthy and vigorous is key.

At Hoʻomaluhia, we also made a management decision that the trees had to survive with little intervention. Maybe koa was not the ideal tree for the Canopy component of the Hawaiian section, Kahua Koa. Some Hoʻomaluhia staffers wanted to just get rid of all of the koa trees, but I wanted to find koa selections that might survive and thrive, and also some horticultural measures that would be feasible in a large garden with a small staff. Many of the koa have died but we still have some of the original trees, plus later plantings. Later plantings from smaller sizes (dibble tubes up to one gallon pots) seemed to work better than the large trees in 50-gallon drums.

Although most of the trees only lived for ten years, some of the wood from dead trees was excellent, dark and curly. We had a volunteer woodworker and he turned a lovely bowl from the wood of a tree that died after only ten years in the ground.

Other Koa in Landscaping

We grew koa at the Honolulu Zoo (1984–87) using innovative techniques. We planted koa in a large leftover sewer pipe filled with the finest "zoo-doo" (elephant manure is a winner!) mixed with composted topsoil. The zoo is at just about zero elevation being next to Waikiki Beach. Amending the soil, raising it above the coralline substrate, supplemental irrigation and pest control helped this tree live.

We planted several young trees as memorials at the Hale Koa Hotel/Fort DeRussy in 1999. These koa trees were grown in our Hale Koa nursery, from seeds collected at low elevations on Oʻahu. We grew them to one-gallon pot size, about five feet tall, and planted into raised beds of rich soil under a large monkeypod tree. They get irrigated automatically every night while the visitors are fast asleep.

These koa were planted in honor of long time Hale Koa gardener Ferdinand Dequilla and "Brother Iz" Israel Kamakawiwoʻole. Some of the last words from this famous Hawaiian musician were *"Plant me a koa tree; don't you cry for me,"* so we did.

Patrick Baker

Silviculturalist, USDA Forest Service, Hawaiʻi

Almost by definition managing forests involves some degree of uncertainty. It's like aiming at a moving target—something is always changing—whether it is the social value of the forest or the market value of the wood products. The primary challenge facing us is whether we can balance economic returns with the conservation of native Hawaiian forests.

My task is to lay down some of the scientific groundwork—to create a foundation of research so that we can learn what works and doesn't work for managing koa forests.

Patrick Baker at Keauhou Ranch

The first thing that I did when I came here was to identify the holes in the knowledge base and identify research opportunities to try to fill them. The problem is, when it comes to data on koa, there are lots of holes! There is remarkably little data about the growth and dynamics of native or managed koa forests.

Although many details remain to be clarified, the "standard" silvicultural approach for koa projects has been to scarify a site using a bulldozer, let seedlings come up, thin out trees, then clearcut. However, after bulldozing the koa seedlings often come up very densely. In dense stands koa trees just do not grow well. They are shade intolerant trees, and they start competing for light and other resources quickly when grown at such high densities. The crowns become thin, growth slows—practically stopping—and trees begin to die.

After just a few years (2–5 years), these types of stands need to be thinned. When a stand is too dense, koa just won't grow. In fact, we recently remeasured 45 study plots in this type of koa stand, at the The Nature Conservancy's Honomolino property in South Kona. We found that the average growth rate of the trees was about 3.5 millimeters (0.14 inches) per year. Essentially, these trees were not growing, because they were so overcrowded. We're just not going to get marketable wood that way.

We have recently started a thinning trial to see how well koa trees in these stands respond when we reduce the stand density to different levels, ranging from 200 trees/hectare (80 trees/acre) up to 900 trees/hectare (360 trees/acre). The current stand density averages 1,500–10,000 trees per hectare (600–4,000 trees/acre). We are hoping that the trees respond. If they don't it will be an important cautionary tale about the problems of overstocked stands.

We're also working to develop alternative models for koa forest regeneration that can meet both conservation and economic goals. The "standard" approach of bulldozer scarification might not be an economically viable option for some landowners interested in establishing koa forests. Not everyone can carry the costs of bulldozing, conducting one or two pre-commercial thinnings, and then wait 40 years until the first harvest. Another drawback to the bulldozer scarification approach is that the growth rate of the trees slows down quickly in the dense stands that result. It is crucial to thin in time. As a silviculturalist, I don't like to see a project that is locked into having to do something that is extremely time-dependent. What if, when the time comes to thin, the project doesn't have the money or the time to do it? What if they don't get to it? The stand may get to a point where it can no longer respond to thinning and the project may be stuck with a lot of small koa that are not going to grow. Overstocked stands of small diameter trees rarely meet any management objectives (e.g., wood production, native bird habitat, aesthetic values, carbon sequestration).

In terms of tree form, some of the nicest examples of young koa that I have seen are found alone or in small groups in the middle of a clump of 'ohi'a. In my experience, when koa grows in dense thickets, very few individuals have good form (i.e., straight stems and well formed crowns). Again, I think that the most important thing to remember when managing for koa is to avoid high densities.

Koa trees in dense stands compete with each other, greatly slowing growth. *Left:* In this stand, koa were so crowded they were growing less than 0.15 inches a year. *Right:* An area that is being thinned to give much more space to relatively few trees.

One approach for regenerating koa that I am interested in is enrichment plantings (planting seedlings into forest gaps). For some landowners this might be a more efficient and cost-effective way to re-establish koa. Little or no thinning would be required, just enough maintenance to get the koa over the grass. The trick is to identify how large the gaps in the forest need to be to ensure that the koa have enough light and space. Interplanting koa with other trees and shrubs that they can eventually outgrow, such as naio or a'ali'i, may be another way to establish koa-dominated forest.

Patrick Baker shows an enrichment planting, koa growing with 'ohi'a

Other silvicultural alternatives for managing koa might involve variations in species mix, density, and/or uniformity of spacing; timing and intensity of thinning, which affects growth rates, tree vigor, and future stand structure; and retaining a proportion of the canopy trees at harvest, which can have important consequences for wildlife habitat, seed availability, wood quality, and economic returns.

For me, there isn't a specific silvicultural system that is the "correct" approach for koa. One system is never going to meet everyone's needs. How you manage your land depends on a variety things: what your management objectives are, what resources (e.g., time and money) you are willing to invest in your land, and the current condition of your land. We'd like to develop a range of silvicultural practices for koa forests that meet both economic and conservation goals. That way landowners have more options available to them. And, I hope, this will get more people involved in growing koa forests in Hawai'i.

Bart Potter

Owner, C. Barton Potter Co. (produces tonewoods of Hawai'i-grown woods for instrument makers worldwide)

I'd like to give an example that, while more anecdotal than scientific, is a firsthand account of how fast and with what quality an *Acacia koa* tree can grow.

I had the extreme good fortune to have been raised on the mountain now called Tantalus situated behind Honolulu. When my parents bought the 1,400 foot elevation, west-facing property in 1951, it had many koa trees on it that, when we thought about it at all, we presumed were natural forest. The trees were already mature in 1950; in fact, as I was growing up, it was not uncommon to hear a large koa fall over in the forest nearby. More often than not, the fallen tree had been overgrown by heavy *Philodendron* vines while still standing which not only contributed weight to the tree but, once established in the crown, weakened the tree by competing for light. As I grew older I began to realize that the forest around us was dynamic and ever-changing. An early ignorance of the extraordinary event taking place under my nose gave way to an amateur passion for learning more about Hawai'i's planted forests and about the growth of koa.

As part of this process I have encountered photographs of Tantalus taken in the mid to late 1800's and early 1900's that show a Tantalus largely devoid of any sizeable trees. Historical accounts also point out that the area behind Honolulu was heavily impacted by the browsing of wild cattle and by the actions of humans collecting firewood for use by city dwellers and visiting ships. By the mid

1870's the Hawaiian government recognized the need to reforest the denuded upslope lands to stem erosion.

Bart Potter with fallen tree on Round Top, O'ahu, harvested with a permit (photo: David Higa)

Government plantings began in the 1880's for which few specific documents can be found but more recent records survive indicating that, as part of ongoing major reforestation efforts involving hundreds of native and introduced species, between the years of 1914 and 1939 government-initiated projects planted over 380,000 koa in various locations on O'ahu. Of these there were around 16,000 planted in the general area of the small plot that was to become my parent's property. Though to be sure there was a local koa population to be found in the Koolau and Waianae mountains, one interesting notation recounts that collected seed from Big Island koa was dumped randomly into a drum that was kept in the Makiki baseyard for forestry operations and dipped into by the O'ahu seedling growers.

Adjoining my parents' property there are single-species stands of other reforestation trees (specifically, brush box (*Lophostemon confertus*) and swamp mahogany (*Eucalyptus robusta*)). Based on the existence of these reforestation stands, the old accounts and photos, and especially the unsung growth capabilities of koa that I have witnessed firsthand (OK, eucalyptus is faster), I hypothesize that the koa on their property was, indeed, planted. It was likely to have been part

of one of the documented plantings that took place in that area of Tantalus between 1920 and 1934 or might have been part of the missing-document plantings prior to that.

During the late 1970's and early 1980's, many O'ahu koa were dying with unusual rapidity. The deaths were characterized by a wilt now identified as being precipitated by the fungus *Fusarium oxysporum* var *koae*—this has prompted the research and attention this problem is now receiving.

At this writing all the old koa trees on my parents' property are gone. Many other koa that I have gathered information on and have reason to believe were planted have also fallen or been swallowed by *Ficus* trees. Thus, an entire generation of planted koa has almost passed, largely undocumented.

Story of a Koa Tree

(Photos by Bart Potter unless otherwise noted.)

This series of photos documents points in the life and "afterlife" of a koa that volunteered around 1983 from seed in the ground at the home of my parents on Tantalus, falling down in November of 2000. It grew on a well-maintained garden slope that receives direct sun from around 11 am to sunset. When my wife Bibiana and I were married in 1987 and the tree was approximately four years old, it was already 15 feet tall, and around six inches in diameter at breast height (DBH). When a sibling growing next to it died a couple years later, the surviving koa really took off. In the late 1990's the tree began to show signs of stress and developed a flush of juvenile leaflets concurrently with the phyllodes. In November of 2000 the tree fell over—three of four lateral roots appeared to have been compromised by rot. In eighteen years the tree had grown to 22" DBH (inside the bark). The main trunk was over six feet long. Whether there was some injury to the tree that caused the damage to the roots during that time we don't know for sure. In the cut faces there was evidence of the *Fusarium*

Left: Bart and Bibiana Potter married near volunteer koa trees in 1987 (Photo: Annie Rogers); *Left center:* Close-up of koa tree and sibling taken around the time of the wedding; *Right center:* A year or two after the wedding photo, the left of the two young trees died of Fusarium wilt; *Right:* Tree in the mid-nineties with hat for scale (nod to Joseph Rock)

fungus mentioned above, though the tree did not seem to be suffering from wilt and was in full leaf when it fell over.

Because of the difficult location in which the tree fell and because my business caters to guitar and ukulele makers, I diced the tree into portable chunks which I transported to my Povlsen bandsaw mill (which has a 5" wide 1/8" kerf blade powered by an Isuzu diesel engine) and then re-sawed into two inch quartersawn lumber for air drying.

In the photo of the fresh-cut board sitting clamped in the dogs of the sawmill, "wetwood", that is, wood that is still sound but which the tree alters in an effort to compartmentalize injury, can be seen as a dark area along the upper edge of the board. To the right of the wetwood is advanced rot associated with the root injury and the interface between them is clearly defined by a

line of "spalt." The sawmill photo also reveals the quality of the good wood: curly throughout, even in the sapwood, with attractive long-running stripes. This photo also shows the yellow color of the fresh cut that later gives way to reds and oranges as the wood reacts to air and light.

I do not yet have any photos of woodwork made from this wood. However, a guitar made out of wood from another Tantalus tree which was significantly older with strikingly similar wood shows what can be achieved. Items made from our tree will have the appearance of the Smart guitar pictured.

This 18 year-old tree represents to me the "Holy Grail" of koa—fast growing, good trunk form and genes predisposed to produce highly figured wood. I retrieved enough wood from that tree to build approximately 25 guitars, a couple rocking chairs and a slew

Left: A sign of stress, the tree flushed out with juvenile leaflets in the late 1990's; *Left Center:* With three of four main lateral roots diseased, the tree fell over in November 2000—Bart's mom Gail and sister Abby lend a sense of scale; *Right Center:* Fallen tree diced into portable chunks; *Right:* The main trunk was 22 inches diameter at breast height (inside the bark)

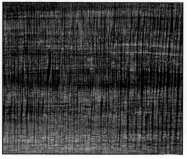

Left: Shows wood quality at time of milling; *Center:* The appearance of the wood after exposure to air, with water applied to accentuate the color; *Right:* Guitar made from similar Tantalus koa by A. Lawrence Smart, of McCall Idaho (photo: Doug Mastaler)

of ukulele and bowls. The planting of koa makes good ecological sense, is very "pono" and is just plain one of the better accomplishments one can hope to achieve. The tree also illustrates that in a best case scenario a reasonable preliminary payback can be expected in 20 years (a very short time for a high value hardwood) and a phenomenal payback could be expected over a 30 to 40 year rotation involving several acres of trees. Koa planted now of good stock would be extremely valuable at maturity.

My parents' property now boasts several koa trees between four and ten years old, both from seed we have planted and from seed-bank volunteers. They are gamely enduring competition from kukui, banyan, bamboo, heliocarpus and a host of faster-growing weedy species. Tantalus is no longer the blank slate that it was at the turn of the last century.

As an aside, a viable seed bank exists in most places where koa has grown during the last 100 years or so, but when an old koa tree falls there is a flush of koa seedlings that are soon outpaced by other plants. In the presence of so many pests, human management of the weedier species is the only chance koa has to get its crown above the crowd and thrive. On O'ahu, in places where weedy pests have a firm foothold, shade-intolerant koa doesn't have a chance in the wild.

As has been pointed out by many working with koa, there is an abundance of oppor-

tunity to improve on the way koa has been selected and grown in the past, as well as opportunity to expand the koa resource. Many koa trees that find their way to market at this time are well beyond their prime, contain lots of rot and are born of entirely random genetic makeup. My hope is that in the not too distant future, the koa seedlings planted by today's adventuresome, culture- and-science-savvy, visionary investor-planters will be abundant enough that healthy koa trees of predictable size and character can be harvested in their prime in perpetuity. Koa is so genetically diverse and the variations in wood character are so pleasing that the work of collecting, analyzing and testing representative genetic material will go on for a long time. Cloning of koa is not far off but I suggest that the job is not over with the creation of one superclone. The ultimate goal may well be to celebrate the diversity inherent in the natural population while breeding out undesirable characteristics, thereby creating a wide range of high quality cultivars.

Real strides can be made in very immediate, low-tech ways in the form of planting from seed of trees of worthy form and/or character. My own preliminary experience and that of others indicates that it is not uncommon for seed of a given koa tree to produce offspring with similar qualities.

I entreat you to have courage—go forth boldly and plant koa!

J. B. Friday

Extension Forester, College of Tropical Agriculture and Human Resources, University of Hawai'i at Manoa

Productivity

We know some things about koa productivity. In Kona, where there is a matrix of ash-derived soils and lava soils, ash-derived soils are better than lava soils. Koa productivity is higher on a'a lava soils than on soils over pahoehoe.

Productivity of koa is probably limited by three main things:

1 In moderately dry to dry areas, water is the biggest influence in the productivity of koa. Drier sites are less productive. In areas that receive more than about 100 inches of rainfall a year, productivity is limited by light or nutrients, not water. Koa trees are adapted to local climates, so koa seeds that comes from trees growing in a drought-prone areas probably result in trees that are more tolerant of drought. Grass competes with trees for moisture, especially in areas that have frequent, light rains, so management of grass around trees may reduce water competition and improve the trees' growth.

2 Since koa is a nitrogen-fixing legume, nitrogen (N) is generally not a factor limiting growth. But phosphorus (P) might be. It's not proven yet, but it might make a difference.

3 In dense stands, growth of an individual koa tree is constrained by its neighbors, so thinning of overcrowded stands is important. The stand biomass may be steadily increasing, but any given tree may only be growing slowly, since there are so many trees. Thinning of koa is an art more than a science. Since koa trees are so valuable, it works best to select the straightest and fastest-growing trees in a stand and "release" these by culling out the other trees competing with them. It is probably only worthwhile to thin out trees with crowns competing with your crop trees (dominant and co-dominant trees). Removing trees which are already overtopped (intermediate and suppressed trees) probably won't help the crop trees. However, sometimes we might choose to remove a larger diameter tree that has a fork or otherwise poor form, and leave a smaller diameter tree that has a good straight form.

JB Friday measuring 27 year-old koa tree with a 26 inch diameter trunk (photo: Brent Sipes)

A big question is how long do you let the stand develop before thinning. In the tropics, lots of thinning is usually recommended where labor is cheap, such as in many developing countries. In Hawai'i, labor is expensive. So, we have to ask: what can we not do? In koa stands, the crowns of neighboring trees with grow together and touch each other in somewhere from four to eight years, depending on how dense the original stand was. After that, the trees grow taller and taller but the amount of leaf area remains constant. The branchy crowns of the trees make up a smaller and smaller fraction of the total height of the tree as the tree grows taller. In general, when the top one-third of the trees is live crown, that's a good time to thin. If trees get too tall and spindly, they will not be able to respond to thinning by growing more rapidly.

Seed Source

If you are on a site where there is koa growing, it's best to collect seeds from what's there. Select seed from individual trees that are straight, healthy, and have been growing well. If you select seed from low, branchy trees because it's easier to get, you will probably grow low, branchy trees. If no koa is present, use the best selections you can get. Go for local populations whenever possible: adaptation to the site and disease resistance trump all other qualities. Disease resistance is of paramount importance. For example, koa wilt (*Fusarium oxysporum* f sp *koae*) is a disease that blocks off the vascular system. Below 2,000 feet elevation on former sugarcane land on the Big Island Fusarium infects most koa plantations. In an experimental site in Pa'auilo Mauka on the Big Island, 70% of the koa seedlings have become infected with the fungus and most have died. We don't know if the fungus has mutated and become more virulent, or if the site conditions can lead to increased outbreaks. Disease resistance is of paramount importance in considering the seed source.

Low elevation plantings

Koa does not generally live long below about 2,000 feet elevation on the windward sides of the islands. In the warmer lowland climates, it tends to flourish at first but then succumb to pests and diseases after five to ten years. There are a few stands of healthy koa which occur at lower elevations, but it's still speculative as to whether these trees have a genetic resistance to pests and diseases that they can pass along. I like to tell tree farmers that planting koa above 2,000 feet is an investment, but below 2,000 feet it's an experiment. Koa is also limited in its usefulness as a landscape tree

except in upcountry areas such as Volcano or Waimea. Where there's an educational value to having a koa tree in the landscape, such as in a native plant garden at a school, growers should expect to have to replace the tree every few years.

Nick Dudley

Research Forester, Hawai'i Agriculture Research Center

Koa is a wildly variable beast. Variations in koa are found in many attributes: growth rate, leaf shape, stem form, wood color, just to name a few. These qualities vary by island, and by elevation within islands.

Wood color, for example, runs a continuum between blonde to chocolate, straight grain to highly figured. This is influenced by genetics, and it can be selected for.

Nick Dudley showing variable koa wood samples

After centuries of reverse genetic selection (harvesting of the best trees) and deforestation, we must assume the genetics of koa have been eroded. Is there a broad enough genetic base left to restore and regenerate koa? I like to think so.

We know that a narrow genetic base can limit koa site adaptability, thus retarding growth and survival. We're early on in the improvement game: it's a broad genetic base, with many parents, and multi-generational in scope.

Planting koa is a bit like going to Las Vegas—it's a risk. The more genetic diversity you have, the better your chance of success. Go with 15–20 or more seed sources. If possible, try to get seed sources within your local ecological zone and from within 1,500 feet of your elevation range. Test them on your site. Based on their performance, expand the outplanting. Planting and managing koa is where art and science meet: what works on one site might not work on another.

Koa is a precious resource and we should take care if it.

Mel Johansen

Land Manager, Honomolino

I grew up here, hunting and helping on the ranch. My dad worked at Manuka State park with all the native plants there, and I have always loved native plants.

The idea now is to replace the cows with sustainable koa forest. In order to help the koa forest thrive, we have to remove the cows and other feral animals including pigs, goats, and sheep. One of my responsibilities is fencing and animal control. We've set up fences. We've gotten the goats and cows out. We managed to catch about 95% of the pigs, but the last 5% are very smart, and they are too wily to catch. That's true with pigs, and with sheep.

Sometimes excluding pigs with fencing and controlling them can bring up controversy in my family. Some relatives will say, "Your great-grandfather hunted pigs! Pigs supported our family, and that's why we're

still here!" I understand that. Certainly, no one is saying to eliminate pigs. In fact, even if that's what everyone wanted, I don't think it would even be possible.

But we do have to look at: what's missing because of the pigs? We can see the understory being damaged terribly by pigs. In the Kau forest edge where there are pigs, there are only 'ohi'a trees, some tree fern, and, rarely, a couple of other natives. And that's about it. Otherwise, all those diverse native understory plants are gone. As someone who loves and knows about native plants, I can see how much is missing. And, what's missing that we don't even know about, destroyed centuries ago by the introduction of pigs? The destruction is incredible. I wonder how many people are aware of it.

Mel Johansen at Honomolino forest

Every three months, a pig can have a litter of twelve piglets. In a drought, maybe only one of those piglets will survive. But in a wet year, all twelve will survive. Every six months, we have to remove at least 70% of the pig population, or the population will increase. So pigs are a real threat.

I think the Mouflon sheep are an even bigger concern for koa. People say Mouflon sheep don't stay in thick forest but they are in there. They are now the biggest threat to koa. In our area, we've tried to get them out, but it's very difficult.

Our goal here is to bring back the koa forest, and that means more than just koa. We want the diversity that comes with it too, the understory plants.

Paul Scowcroft

Senior Forester, USDA Forest Service Institute of Pacific Islands Forestry

Frost

Frost is a real issue for seedling establishment at higher elevations. In open areas, the probability of frost is much higher. If there are trees nearby that are over two meters tall (6 feet), the seedlings probability will suffer less. The canopy of other trees in the are moderates the temperature.

Paul Scowcroft presenting research findings at Keauhou Ranch

Establishment of other natives

Just because we started with bare ground and lots of koa came up, that doesn't mean the forest will just be koa. At Keauhou Ranch, a whole suite of natives has regenerated in the understory, including 'ohi'a, mamaki, pilo, olapa, alani, and naio. It's becoming a very nice, diverse forest. But if invasives such as blackberry move into the area instead, it will affect reestablishment of the koa and other natives. We're looking at how controlling non-natives in the understory helps koa establishment.

Harvest

The theory in a natural koa forest is: when one large tree dies or is removed, another koa tree will come up to take it's place. When the time comes to harvest a koa tree, we want that one to-one replacement.

Kelly Greenwell

Farm Forester, Kona, Hawai'i

Our objective was to recreate a complete forest, a mixture of native species including Koa, rather than an exclusive planting of only Koa. Our concern therefore was for all the various plants which made up the forest and particularly their frequency within the forest.

Interestingly, we found the mature Koa trees occurred at a density of only one tree per acre. This is perhaps mainly due to the fact that cattle were introduced to our forests a hundred and fifty years ago and the Koa, a legume, was virtually the only plant in Hawaiian forests that cattle would eat. Therefore, any seedling that had not attained sufficient stature to keep it out of reach was eaten. Other contributing factors include the variation in terrain, randomly occurring pockets of soil, shade from parent trees, competition from other plants, and diseases and insects which were advantaged by higher densities.

Prior to the restoration effort we removed eighty-one salvageable logs, which had fallen during the last decade, along with a half dozen dead or dying trees. We milled these logs into lumber. which was sold to craftsmen and woodworking artisans whose finished work resulted in over thirty two million dollars being brought into our community.

Kelly Greenwell in koa grove at Honokohau (photo: Lou Lambert)

As we began our restoration efforts, we found that the scarifying of the forest floor, which occurred in the process of dragging the logs out, exposed the ground to sunlight and Koa seedlings sprouted by the thousands.

While we had initially planned to replant, the real effort now switched to thinning. Because we had a cattle background, the idea that they might be an aid occurred to us. Hence, the fencing we installed to keep the cattle out would now find its use in keeping the cattle in.

We brought in young stock because of their tendency to graze rather than browse (they eat with their heads down, whereas older cattle reach up and tear down or trample saplings to get at the foliage) and kept them in for short durations. By using a rotational program the taller trees grew even taller and were further out of harm's way when the cattle returned for the next round.

Today, as a result of this effort, we have not only produced a significant economic impact on our community, we have helped advance the protocol for forestry, and culturally we again have a Koa forest, along with three Koa canoes in the paddling fleet.

As we continue to study our forest, we need to remind ourselves that the Koa has been evolving and adapting to its environment for perhaps millions of years. We have been studying it for less than fifty.

Mark Kimball

Farm Forester, Holualoa

I've been planting koa in Kona in increments of about five acres per year for the past five years. We decide the time of year for planting based on expectations for the beginning of the rainy season. The beginning of rainy season is probably best so that the seedlings don't have to go through an extended dry period soon after planting. Lots of rain means the weeds also grow very fast—I have also had good results planting at end of the rainy season, due to less weed competition.

To prepare for planting in most areas we use a bulldozer to clear away the thick growth of Christmas berry (*Schinus terebinthifolius*), mulang (*Michelia champaca*), and strawberry guava (*Psidium cattleianum*). On our site we have to watch out for thin soil over pahoehoe, as those are poor planting areas for koa. Stands of dense strawberry guava almost always indicate pahoehoe lies underneath. When the bulldozer hits those patches of strawberry guava, the patch just peels off exposing sheets of pahoehoe underneath.

Before planting, I mark out the planting spots with flagging stakes. I start with a handful of flags and walk out to the middle of the field. I sight by eye across the field lay out a line of flags by stepping off an even distance between flags. From this central row I orient subsequent rows. I've learned through experience how to sight along the rows to mark out the planting spots evenly across variable terrain.

Mark Kimball on a new planting at his Kona farm

Regarding the planting density we use, we want plenty of trees to compensate for losses due to poor planting spots, pig damage, etc. On the other hand, we don't want to have to thin out too many trees too soon. We initially planted about 500 trees/acre, which we discovered required cutting down about half the trees within four years. Our current spacing gives about 260 trees/acre.

Generally, we've learned that it's unnecessary to add fertilizer because right after bulldozing there's lots of nutrients available in the organic matter. The trees have done really well 1 to 2 months right after bulldozing, after the organic matter has had a bit of time to decompose. A few weeks after planting, we supplement nutrient-poor areas.

For the first two months I check the new planting about once week. I do that to make sure something hasn't stepped on, or pushed over trees. I walk down the rows to upright seedlings that are at an angle or laying down. I want them to be nice and straight from the beginning.

Pigs are a big problem, as they like to bite off or dig under seedlings. Overspraying with herbicide by inexperienced workers is a bigger problem—we've suffered more loses from errant herbicide than the pigs ever killed. Stem borers are a problem as well. Koa often dies back from the borer. I've had trees 1–2 inches in diameter die back to within a foot of

the ground. Some of these, after being cut back to below the borer damage have come back and have continued to grow borer free. Water-stressed trees growing in loose rock seem to be most susceptible to borer attack.

Someday we're going to find koa trees that are more resistant to borers and others pests; just keep planting and we're going to find some eventually. Small landowners will come up with improvements by trial and error, something we haven't thought of yet.

Kanoa Kimball

Farm Forester, Holualoa

I really like growing koa because it is a native tree. We've planted it together with many different introduced hardwoods such as mahogany and red cedar in areas which were disturbed and did not have any native plants. I would like to also plant koa in some undisturbed kipuka which have some of the other native plants from koa's natural ecosystem.

Kanoa Kimball with year old seedling at his Kona farm (1,700 feet elevation)

For the first couple of years, we planted trees that had not been inoculated with nitrogen fixing bacteria. After that, we've only planted inoculated trees. The inoculated trees grew much faster and seemed to resist the stem borer much better.

We've also started planting trees from selected parents. There seem to be some varieties that have much better form than others.

I know it's not recommended to prune koa, but we prune the small trees to avoid overspray from herbicide when they're young.

The big problem we've had is with pigs. They bite off the tops of small koa seedlings, and tear off strips of bark on older koa seedlings. What I would do differently in the future is to sit up in the new forest and hunt out the pigs. Pig eradication is very important.

Sally Rice

Vice President, AgroResources Inc.
Director, Hawai'i Forest Industry Association

Planning is an essential aspect of growing koa. When we have a project that is going to plant koa trees, we start to plan immediately. The seedlings will have to be ordered in advance, so we have to look at the project and decide what's required. We figure out spacing, land preparation, and management strategies. We plan ahead of time before ordering the seedlings, and then we do a lot more work planning and preparing the site before we actually get trees and put them in ground. Advance planning and preparation is key to the success of the project.

The source of the koa seedlings is very important. In past years, I have planted koa seedlings from random seed selections and have also seen koa seedlings on other projects that were planted from random seed. More recently, we've been planting trees from elite tree selections done by a local nursery.

The difference in performance is night and day—it's astounding. Koa trees from the random seed collections are usually bushy and short. Also, they tend not be very thrifty. For example, on some sites they seem to run out of energy, and sometimes even die or are out-competed by the surrounding vegetation.

In contrast, trees from select seed grow very straight and tall. In general they have few side branches, and are often self-pruning. They grow very well. There is no doubt in my mind that getting the best plant material is crucial to the success of the project.

Sally Rice examines newly planted koa

We've also done some side-by-side trials of different select seed sources. We're not far enough along to make exact conclusions, but there is definitely an environmental issue in planting koa. In other words, koa grown from seed from one area may do very well on one site, but not so well on another site. So we know that besides using seedlings from elite seeds, we want some concept of our environment and where the seed source came from so we can make the best match for the site.

Land preparation and the methods of weed control are especially important to figure out in advance. We have to look at the land and decide what's needed as far as preparation. Sometimes it will be major, for example on a site with Christmas berry. If people have heavy brush, I strongly recommend grinding or chipping to put the organic matter back on the land. There are all kinds of different challenges, but whether it is guava, guinea grass, sugarcane, Christmas berry, or whatever, my advice is: get it well under control *before* you plant any trees.

Another key subject is weed control after the trees are planted. In Hawai'i, with our warm year-round climate, we have to be vigilant about weed control. It is essential to keep the grass and weeds away from the koa trees, especially during the first year or two. This is a real challenge, and should not be underestimated. You have to be so careful with that early maintenance and stay right on top of it, keeping the grass away from the trees and at the same time making sure not to affect the trees with any herbicide drift. It is very hard, especially to do it economically. We have to carefully analyze each situation and have a good plan for keeping the weeds under control.

As far as fertilizing, we like to get a soil sample in advance of planting, especially to look at the pH and any mineral deficiencies. Phosphorus is very important, and there are some other common deficiencies such as calcium or magnesium. If we are able, we like to amend the soil prior to planting, especially on sites that have poor fertility. When we plant the trees, we also use a mild 8–8–8 fertilizer. This gives the tree a little boost, but is simple to apply and we don't have to worry that it will damage the tree.

From then on, we base any future fertilizing on the soil analysis. Every place is different. Some areas require more fertilizer or more frequency of fertilizing than others. After the first year, we amend once or twice a year, if the project's budget allows. There is no question in my mind that fertilization is important, especially for the first few years, if you are going to do commercial forestry.

In other ongoing maintenance, pigs are a problem when they come in to an area. A perfect world scenario is to put up a pig-proof fence around the perimeter prior to planting. It doesn't have to be too high, just the small standard size hog wire fence (lightweight wire is fine) with two strands of barbed wire at the base. One of the barbed wires should be right on the ground, and another about four inches up, so the pig will be blocked when it tries to put its snout under the hog wire. As long as the fence is tight and properly installed, it works well. However, some projects simply can't afford a pig-proof fence. In that case, pigs can be controlled by trapping and hunting.

Last, I would also recommend that anyone thinking of growing koa either for native forest restoration or for commercial timber talk to the people who are presently involved in doing research in koa. It is always good to talk to people who are involved in hands-on research. You will get some good information.

Ernest Pung

Ernest Pung, retired Service Forester, State Division of Forestry and Wildlife

During the years 1948–59 I was a Forest Ranger on Hualalai (North Kona). This started before Hawai'i was a state; even at that time the Territory of Hawai'i had a Division of Forestry. I used to ride a pack mule from the main highway up to our cabin, which took four and a half hours. I stayed in the cabin all week. Above 3,000 feet elevation there were koa trees everywhere, upright, healthy trees. There were plenty of alala (Hawaiian crows), flocks of up to twenty. I remember a number of years later, koa would lose their branches, and fall over. When you go up now, all those big trees have fallen down. I don't believe anyone logged up there, but it's all gone now. The trees died on their own and are gone through natural attrition.

I have a strong hunch that climatic changes have occurred, and that was the downfall of the koa. The total rainfall may not have changed drastically. However, where we used to get rainfall year-round in the koa area, there are more prolonged, and frequent droughts, and the koa are suffering. Also, the moisture brought in by daily fog has diminished.

There's no question that cattle love koa; they consume it like crazy. If there's cattle loose in the area, you've got to erect a damn good fence that will keep them out, and then maintain it for 20 years. Cows grab hold of the bark, and strip it right off the tree. They prefer the early smooth bark phase in younger koa, so they should be kept away from the trees until they are a minimum age of 15–20 years.

In my opinion, there are two koa belts: the lower belt below 3,000 feet, and the upper belt between 3,000–9,500 feet. In my experience in the lower belt, 80% of lumber is yellowish-white, and therefore not very valuable. In the higher elevations, the tendency is for nice dark colors, and higher density wood. For a timber investment, planting koa in lower elevations is a very risky business. However, if planting koa at lower elevations for environmental purposes, I say go for it.

Peter D. Simmons

Senior Land Manger, Kamehameha Schools

We started out trying to see if we could grow canoe logs of koa. But now we have wider, expanded values. Instead of pure stands of koa, we see an abundance of opportunities for future generations: cultural, educational, wildlife, birds. How do we define the value?

Peter Simmons at Keauhou Ranch

One land manager in one lifetime is not going to make all the decisions and learn all that needs to be learned. What people have with koa is a multi-generational kinship relationship with a living organism. It demands being multi-generational. Research transects should be there for hundreds of years.

A koa seedling is like a child. We can start out with a great seedling, but it also needs a good environment to thrive.

We're learning how to reforest better and better.

Roger G. Skolmen

Principal Silviculturist (retired), USDA Forest Service

Koa is capable of growing over a much larger range on the Island of Hawai'i than the range it presently occupies. Koa can be replaced in its former habitat. There are several examples of how this can be achieved, including Bishop Estate's reforestation project at Keauhou. For commercial ventures, costs of reforesting with koa appear to be prohibitive.

Although presently there is no serious threat to the continued presence of koa as a species, there is a threat to the continued presence of the large diameter, long stemmed koa trees that are preferred for timber. This is not because this type is being logged off so fast, but rather because this type has not and is not being replaced either naturally or artificially.

Koa, in order to grow, needs a certain amount of precipitation. As a very young seedling it needs water almost daily; three or four days of drought can kill it. Later, it can survive two or three months without rain if it is one of those trees that has always grown in a uniformly wet area, and it can survive six months of drought if it originated in an area of frequent drought and adapted itself to the site by growing a deeper root system. With trees we can't just be concerned with mean or annual rainfall, we have to be concerned also with minimum rainfall, because it is the minimum years that result in the absence of trees from a landscape.

The amount of rainfall required to grow koa varies with temperature, which in turn is controlled largely by elevation. On the Big Island, the best koa forests, those with 5 or 6 tall straight trees per acre, are located just below the usual position of the temperature inversion that limits cloud height on the mountain slopes. On the windward slopes of Mauna Kea and Mauna Loa, this lies between 4,000 and 6,500 feet (1,219 and 1,981 m) as far north as Keanakolu and today rises to between 5,000 and 6,500 feet (1524 and 1961 m) for some distance north of Keanakolu. The average annual rainfall throughout the area where the tall dense forest grows is about 85 inches (2,159 mm), varying from 65 to 125 inches (1,651 to 3,175 mm), with almost daily cloud cover for a portion of the day, and droughts rarely exceeding two months in any year.

Proceeding north from Keanakolu around the mountain is a large area of pasture between 3,000 and 6,000 feet (914 and 1,829 m) that presently supports the savanna type of koa with short stems and spreading crowns. This is largely because the rainfall in that area is too low, droughts are too frequent and lengthy, and desiccating winds are too strong to support a dense forest. Before cattle destroyed it, the forest in this area was considerably denser than the present precipitation can support. This may be because the loss of tree cover caused a warming of the air passing over, resulting in slightly less cloud cover, less precipitation in that immediate area, and thus an inability to maintain a large cover of trees.

On the Kona side, starting on the north slope of Hualalai, and proceeding south, the koa belt is now and always was confined to those patches of deep a'a flows and patches of deep soil formed on or near cinder deposits between 3,500 and 6,500 feet (1,067 and 1,981 m). In Kona, because of the almost perennial formation of heavy cloud cover in mid-morning, tall, dense forest of koa grow

with less rainfall than on the windward slopes. Although most of the present and former koa forest was in a 65 to 85 inch (1,651 and 2,159 mm) rainfall zone, in some of the deep soil cinder areas dense, tall forest occurred with rainfall as low as 40 inches (1,016 mm). I attribute the presence of the forest to the almost daily wet, heavy cloud cover.

In Ka'u, mauka (upslope) of Kapapala Ranch headquarters, is a patch of essentially pristine, pure koa forest at the upper 6,540 feet (1,993 m) edge which gradually changes into mixed koa-ohia and then straight ohia forest as one comes downhill. The rainfall at the upper boundary is about 50 inches (1,270 mm) with a Kona type of daily cloud cover increasing to about 85 inches (2,159 mm) lower down where koa drops out in favor of ohia. On fairly recent lava flows, where the soils are Histosols or organic muck, koa is found in certain areas.

Below 2,000 feet (610 m) on the windward side, we find koa growing again in spots with deep soil. In fact, the first sawmill we know of was located very close to Hilo In such a low elevation patch of koa. I believe koa grew in gullies and perhaps on ridges in patches between about 1,000 and 2,000 feet (305 and 610 m) all along the Hamakua coast and that some of this was large sawtimber. Bates' (1854) description of the forest between Hanaiopoe and Waipio as an "immense forest of koa" lends support to this theory. If true, all the land mauka of Honokaa and Kukuihaele would have been this dense koa forest. The rainfall and soil in this area would be ideal, although today in the pastures above Ahualoa, the only native tree present is ohia, with no evidence of koa stumps.

The first Europeans to look at the Hamakua coast from the sea describe it as grass covered to about 2,000 feet (610 m) with trees in the gullies. I think they overstated the elevation based on present evidence, but probably the grass was the result of Hawaiians burning off the forest to create cropland. I had originally left koa out of a windward portion of the Waimea plain where many think it grew. I thought the many years of extreme drought that this plain suffers would preclude it as a koa site. But Irving Jenkins was able to show me three separate citations of people who described the koa forests of this area. So it was there, and it was koa.

Koa can be replaced in areas where it once grew.

(This perspective was adapted from Skolmen 1986.)

Rob Pacheco

Naturalist, Hawai'i Forest & Trail

It is a big tree. It rises above the canopy of the kipuka with sculptured grace. Its trunk is as thick as a bus. The branches are larger than most other trees' trunks. It is a Koa. I visit the tree often, with hundreds of visits over the years. Only after a dozen visits did I see how expansive its crown truly spread. Nearly every visit brings a new discovery at this great creature. It is ancient and noble. And it is generous. The life that exists on, around, and in this monarch of the forest is remarkable. The tree is more than just itself, it is the sum of all that make it their home. This koa contains a priceless inventory of life.

Nearly 25 feet in circumference, over 100 feet tall, and with a crown spread close to 150 feet, the koa has plenty of room for all sorts of organisms. The first things I noticed were all the epiphytes. Epiphytes are plants that grow on other plants. In rainforests just about any plant can grow epiphytically including other trees. There is a 20-foot tall 'ōhi'a lehua growing in the crotch of the main fork in the trunk. It's a pretty little 'ohi'a that has a fine perch above the fern floor below. Three other species of trees and shrubs grow on the koa. At its base a half dozen olapa trees, with their antiseptic, turpentine odor, grow on the thick koa roots that crawl along the forest floor. There is also a pukiawe and an ohelo, which take hold next to each other on a large root.

Unlike the small shrubs one finds on the lava flows, these individuals are small trees 10–15 feet tall.

Rob Pacheco enjoying a close encounter with a koa tree and its forest community (photo: Carl Waldbauer)

Ferns, mosses, lichens, molds and fungus account for the great majority of plants on the Koa. About 60 feet high, along a major branch, the shuttlecock fern, *Dryopteris wallichiana* rises up in its distinctive shape of a badminton birdie. Besides the *Dryopteris* there are lots of other ferns sprouting on the koa. Hairy stag's tongue (*Elaphoglossum hirtum*) is perhaps the most numerous. Another Stag's tongue is ekaha, which has a smooth, fleshy stalk unlike its hairy cousin. Two tiny little finger ferns grow in bunches right next to one another, the kolokolo (*Grammitis tenella*) and the small, serrated kihe (*Lellingeria saffordii*). Three different *Asplenium* ferns find moist little crannies to their satisfaction. Many parts of the tree are covered in various mosses. Some are thick and spongy, others are thin and slimy. Most of the upper smaller branches are draped in the yellow, stringy lichen that looks like Spanish moss. There is a bright green mold in one spot of damp shade that appears to be the same stuff that grows so easily on bread in Hawai'i. Below the mold is a large Table-bract fungus. Yellow-white in color, it is smooth and cool to touch and leaves a lovely aromatic mushroom scent on the fingers.

My favorite epiphyte is the ala ala wainui. Its beauty is hidden from casual view. From the top it looks like a plain green plant with small pointed leaves. Turn the leaves over and an exquisite deep variegated maroon color is revealed. Looking up the tree, the ala ala wainui glows with color as the sunlight passes through from above. They are precious, twinkling tree ornaments.

The invertebrate residents of the Koa are numerous. There is a large honeybee hive in a cavity from a broken branch. It is a significant nest with honeycomb visible from the ground and black propolis stains leaking down the trunk. *Plagithmysus varians* is a cute little triangular woodborer whose larvae provide an important food source for some forest birds. The Koa bug (*Coleotichus blackburiae*) is the largest native bug. Its back is dimpled with dots of iridescent green and blue. Spiders are usually easily found among the bark and small cavities. The Long-jawed, hump-backed, spiny-legged spider, (no description needed after the common name!) has the wonderful scientific moniker *Tetragnathus quasimodo*. Though in the orb-weaver family, it has given up building a web and hunts its prey raptorially. Once at night, I discovered the largest spider I've ever seen in the native forest. It was a Comb's footed spider that was

bright rusty orange, just like the orange rusty mold or lichen growing on the tree's bark. Three to three and a half inches in length, its arched abdomen gave off a metallic sheen. I have yet to find one again.

Partly because of the tree's invertebrate wealth, it is a fabulous place for birds. The great Koa has given me hours of enjoyable bird watching. I have observed every bird species found in the forest along its trunks and limbs or foraging among its leaves and flowers. I'o, the Hawaiian hawk has perched in its branches. Family groups of endangered Hawai'i Creepers and the 'akiapola'au have gleaned insects from its wood and bark. 'Amakihi, 'apapane, and 'i'iwi frequent the tree for insects and nectar. 'Oma'o has nested for two seasons within a small hole in a limb. 'Elepaio flit around catching bugs, flies and moths. Turkeys roost for the night as do Kalij pheasant. A Japanese white-eye once took a birdbath in a fresh pool of rainwater caught in a crack of the tree. There are always birds to be found within the koa.

The Koa is a treasure chest in the forest. Its existence provides for a richness of life that is uniquely Hawaiian. Yes, there is value in a koa picture frame, hand-turned bowl, or a handcrafted furniture piece. But how can we value the richness of a living tree?

(This perspective was adapted from Pacheco 1997.)

Chapter 10: Resources

There are books, web sites, government agencies, and organizations that are helpful in learning more about koa and forests.

Expert farmer Kamilo Faleofa shares his mana'o

People

There is no substitute for direct experience. Chances are there is someone nearby planting koa, or perhaps an older person who remembers the history of the area. Many aspiring koa planters don't know how to approach someone whose koa planting they have heard about or seen from a distance. Yet, it is an essential part of learning to meet others in the area and hear about their experiences. These valuable relationships can be a wellspring of information and inspiration, as well as result in long-term supportive friendships. To make it more comfortable, effective and enjoyable, there is a certain code of conduct that goes along with tapping into a tree planter's wealth of information.

1 Do your homework in advance. Before asking someone to take time out from their day to share information with you, be sure you have checked the local resources that provide free information first. The internet and public library system are a rich sources of information. Through this up-front research, you won't have to take up time for basic information that is readily available elsewhere.

2 Be respectful of a grower's time and space. Find out if the grower is willing to have you as visitor. While some tree planters are happy to show off their activities, most are also very busy. Call and ask if they have a couple minutes to talk about what you are interested in. Start a conversation by letting them know how familiar you are with them, such as, "I've been admiring the line of koa trees on the border of your property..." Then, introduce yourself briefly. If the grower does not have a phone, stop by briefly in person for this purpose. Don't expect them to drop what they are doing to show you around; you should stop by first for a few minutes just to see if would be convenient to come back, and if so, to make an appointment for a future visit.

3 Start with a small request, and be specific about what you want to see or talk about. In other words, don't ask, "Can I come over and have a tour of your planting?" which can be a large, time-consuming request to fulfill. Instead say, "I see you are trying an interesting technique to control weeds. I am working on some similar problems. I was wondering if sometime I could stop by for a few minutes and have a quick look at what you are doing?"

4 If the grower is willing, make a firm appointment. Treat the appointment just as you would an appointment with any professional. Be on time. Don't expect the grower to be on time, just be ready when they are.

Some Do's and Don't's of a Tree Planting Visit

Here are a few guidelines to keep in mind during your visit:

Do:

- Arrive on time. Ten minutes early is courteous and relieves doubt about whether or not you will show up. If they are not ready, wait patiently until they are.

- Thank them up front for being willing to see you. Especially if it is an older person, bringing a small gift is a nice way to show appreciation.

- Have a few specific things you want to ask about or see, or a short list of questions.

- Ask for permission if you want to photograph them or their trees.

- Be brief and leave on time or early. Even if you are all having a great time, it is much better to have them wishing you would stay longer than wishing you would leave! If they see that you do in fact respect their time, they'll be glad to have you back again.

- Thank and acknowledge them at the end of your visit. Let them know how much you value their time and knowledge. It is nice for them to sit back for a moment and see through your eyes all that they have accomplished.

- If possible, send a short note or gift to thank them again.

Here are some things to avoid:

- Don't pry if they seem reluctant to discuss certain aspects of their operation. Remember, their planting may also be part of their business and livelihood, and some things may be proprietary, "trade secrets" they may not be ready to share with you.

- Don't focus on or talk about yourself and your own plans while you are there. You'll get the most value if you focus on what they are doing in their situation, and try to apply it to your own later.

- Don't give unsolicited advice. You are there to learn, not to teach. Of course, share your thoughts if asked, but stay in learning mode.

- Don't ask to use their phone, home or bathroom. If you are not a house guest, your request to use private family space may be a burden.

With these few guidelines in hand, hopefully you will be more comfortable approaching that neighbor in your region to learn from their experience. Soon you'll be hooked on cultivating connections with your tree growing neighbors.

Also, do pass it on. If others have shared their experience with you, keep the cycle going by being willing to show others the successes and failures of your planting.

The Hawai'i State Public Library System has nearly all titles listed below

Recommended Reading

Abott, Isabella Aiona. 1992. Lā'au Hawai'i— Traditional Hawaiian Uses of Plants. Bishop Museum Press, Honolulu. With dozens of archival-quality photographs, this volume provides a comprehensive description of how Hawaiians cultivated and used plants.

Beletski, L. 2000. Hawaii: The Ecotravellers' Wildlife Guide. Academic Press, London. An in-depth and richly illustrated guide to Hawai'i's wildlife.

Bornhorst, Heidi Leianuenue. 1996. Growing Native Hawaiian Plants—A How-to Guide for the Gardener, The Bess Press, Honolulu. Gives expert propagation and cultivation advice for many native trees and shrubs.

Burgess, P. (Ed). 1996. From Then to Now: A Manual for Doing Things Hawaiian Style. Ka'ala Farm, Inc., P.O. Box 630, Wai'anae, HI, 96792. A fantastic "starter kit" for anyone who loves Hawai'i.

Clark, W.C. and R.R. Thaman. 1993. Agro-Forestry in the Pacific Islands: Systems for Sustainability, United Nations University Press, Tokyo. Very thorough treatment of agroforestry practices in the Pacific. Includes tables and descriptions of many traditional agroforestry species.

Cuddihy L.W., Stone C.P. 1990. Alteration of Native Hawaiian Vegetation: Effects of Humans, Their Activities, and Introductions. University of Hawai'i, National Park Resources Studies Unit, Honolulu.

Culliney, J.L. 1988. Islands in a Far Sea: Nature and Man in Hawai'i. Sierra Club Books, San Francisco, CA. Traces the natural and human history of the islands and the root causes of current environmental problems.

Dalla Rosa, K. 1994. Acacia koa—Hawaii's most valued native tree (NFTA 94–08). Nitrogen Fixing Tree Association, Morrilton, Arkansas. Web: http://www.winrock.org /forestry/factpub/factsh/akoa.htm. A concise introduction to koa.

Elevitch, Craig R. and Kim M. Wilkinson. 2000. Agroforestry Guides for Pacific Islands. Permanent Agriculture Resources, Holualoa, HI. Series of 22–50 page guides covering eight topics in Pacific Island agroforestry. Web: http://www.agroforestry.net

Elevitch, Craig R. and Kim M. Wilkinson. 2001. The Overstory Book: Cultivating Connections with Trees. Permanent Agriculture Resources, Holualoa, HI. Seventy-two concise, easy to read chapters covering key agroforestry concepts. Web: http://www.overstory.org

Felling, Candace. 2002. Acacia koa botany. Web: http://www.hawaii.edu/gk-12/evolution/candacef.htm. Presents in photos the biological, anatomical, and ecosystem diversity of koa.

Ferentinos, L. and D.O. Evans (Eds). 1997. Koa: A Decade of Growth. Proceedings of the 1996 Annual Symposium held by the Hawaii Forest Industry Association November 18–19, 1996. Contains over 40 papers and presentations.

Friday, J.B. 2000. Seed Technology for Forestry in Hawaii (RM–4). University of Hawai'i, Honolulu. Web: http://www2.ctahr.hawaii.edu/f orestry/Data/publications.html

Gustafson, R. and S.H. Sohmer. 1987. Plants and Flowers of Hawai'i. University of Hawai'i Press, Honolulu. Introduces 130 important native plants of Hawai'i, with color photographs.

Habte, M. and N.W. Osorio. 2001. Arbuscular Mycorrhizas: Producing and Applying Arbuscular Mycorrhizal Inoculum. College of Tropical Agriculture &Human Resources (CTAHR), University of Hawai'i, Honolulu. Answers common questions about AM fungi and provides information that will enable interested individuals to produce and then evaluate inoculants with minimal external assistance.

Handy, E.S. Craighill and Elizabeth G. Handy. 1972. Native Planters of Old Hawai'i: Their Life, Lore, and Environment. Bishop Museum Press, Honolulu. An extremely detailed account of Hawaiian horticulture, ethnobothany and cultural practices.

Holmes, T. 1981. The Hawaiian Canoe. Editions Limited, Hanalei, Hawai'i. Written by one of the founders of the Polynesian Voyaging Society, details not only the forms and functions of Hawaiian canoes and surfboards, but also the traditional tools and processes of canoe building "from the forest to the sea."

Jenkins, Irving. 1983. Hawaiian Furniture and Hawai'i's Cabinet Makers: 1820–1940. Daughters of Hawai'i. Honolulu. A historical survey of Hawaiian furniture making lavishly illustrated with over 300 illustrations, including numerous photographs of koa furniture.

Juvik, Sonia P. and James O. Juvik. Atlas of Hawaiʻi, Third Edition. University of Hawaiʻi Press, Honolulu. The comprehensive reference for Hawaiʻi's physical, biotic, cultural and social environments.

Kepler, Angela Kay. 1984. Hawaiian Heritage Plants, The Oriental Publishing Co., Honolulu. This generously illustrated book covers over 30 native and Polynesian introduced plants.

Krauss, Beatrice H. 1993. Plants in Hawaiian Culture, University of Hawaiʻi Press. Honolulu. With brief descriptions of almost 100 species, this book extensively covers plant use by Hawaiians.

Lamb, Samuel H. 1981. Native Trees & Shrubs of the Hawaiian Islands, Sunstone Press, Santa Fe, NM. A botanical reference for many Hawaiian forest species.

Landis, Tom D, R.W. Tinus, S.E. McDonald, and J.B. Barnett. 1990. The Container Tree Nursery Manual (vols. 1-7). Agriculture Handbook 674. U.S. Dept. of Agriculture Forest Service: Washington, DC. A very useful nursery manual for growing trees for reforestation.

Little, Elbert L. and Roger G. Skolmen. 1989. Common Forest Trees of Hawaiʻi (Native and Introduced). United States Department of Agriculture Forest Service, Agriculture Handbook 679. Describes over 150 common forestry species from the perspective for forestry production.

Mollison, Bill and Reny Mia Slay. 1991. Introduction to Permaculture. Tagari Publishers, Tyalgum, Australia. A concise and easy-to-read introduction to designing gardens, farms and forests.

Mollison, Bill. 1997. Permaculture: A Practical Guide for a Sustainable Future. Ten Speed Press, Berkeley, California. The premiere guide to designing resource systems in harmony with natural processes.

Nagata, K.M. 1992. How to Plant a Native Hawaiian Garden. Office of Environmental Quality Control, Honolulu, HI 96813. Only available in public and school libraries, this handbook is very helpful to those interested in establishing a native Hawaiian garden.

Neal, Marie C. 1965. In Gardens of Hawaiʻi, Bishop Museum Press, Honolulu. This classic and encyclopedic volume describes hundreds of species found in Hawaiʻi, and their uses.

Rock J.F. 1913. The Indigenous Trees of the Hawaiian Islands, 1st ed. Honolulu: Priv. published. 2nd ed. 1974. Charles E. Tuttle, Tokyo. A richly illustrated volume by the father of Hawaiian botany; a seemingly timeless reference about Hawaiian forests.

Staples, G.W., and R.H. Cowie. 2001. Hawaiʻi's Invasive Species. Mutual Publishing and Bishop Museum Press, Honolulu. An excellent introduction to a wide variety of invasive species and the problems caused by each.

Wadsworth, Frank H. 1997. Forest Production for Tropical America. United States Department of Agriculture Forest Service, Agriculture Handbook 710. An excellent introduction to forestry, emphasizing timber production.

Wagner W.L., Herbst D.R., Sohmer S.H. 1999. Manual of the Flowering Plants of Hawaiʻi, Revised edition. University of Hawaiʻi Press, Honolulu. An encyclopedic reference to plants in Hawaiʻi.

Whitesell, Craig D. 1990. Acacia koa A. Gray. In: Burns, R.M., Honkala, B. Silvics of North America Vol. 2: Hardwoods. USDA Forest Service Agricultural Handbook No. 654, 17–28. Very good silvicultural reference for koa.

Agencies

The Cooperative Extension Service (CES) of the University of Hawaiʻi can assist landowners with questions relating to koa. Has an excellent web site for forestry including many valuable publications, forestry news, and an extensive list of forestry links for Hawaiʻi. Also organizes helpful field days. Contact:

Extension Forester
College of Tropical Agriculture and Human Resources
University of Hawai'i at Manoa
Komohana Agricultural Complex
875 Komohana St., Hilo, HI 96720
Tel: 808-959-9155; Fax: 808-959-3101
Web: http://www2.ctahr.hawaii.edu/forestry

Several government agencies offer assistance with forest establishment and conservation

The State of Hawai'i Department of Land and Natural Resources Division of Forestry and Wildlife provides information, education, and support for forestry. Some cost-sharing programs and other partnerships with private landowners are available. Contact:

Division of Forestry and Wildlife
1151 Punchbowl St. Room 325
Honolulu, HI 96813-3089
Tel: 808-587-0166, Fax: 808-587-0160
Web: http://www.hawaii.gov/dlnr/dofaw/

The Natural Resources Conservation Service (NRCS), formerly the Soil Conservation Service) provides assistance with conservation practices such as windbreaks and contour plantings. They also have a Forest Incentive Program, to increase the supply of timber products from nonindustrial private forest lands. The NRCS has offices throughout the US including Hawai'i and the American-affiliated Pacific. To find a nearby office contact:

NRCS State Office
P.O. Box 50004
Honolulu, HI 96850-0050

Tel: 808-541-2600
Fax: 808-541-1335 or 541-2652
Web: http://www.hi.nrcs.usda.gov

Institute of Pacific Islands Forestry develops and implements programs to restore, protect, and sustain upland and wetland forests of the Pacific for purposes of conservation and utilization. Includes assistance programs for individuals and communities:

Institute of Pacific Islands Forestry
1151 Punchbowl Street, Room 323
Honolulu, HI 96813
Tel: 808-522-8230; Fax: 808-522-8236
Web: http://ipif.psw.fs.fed.us/

The Forest TEAM Program at Hawai'i Community College trains students to actively manage threatened native forests and the regeneration of Hawai'i's native ecosystems.

Forest TEAM Program
Email: forteam@hawaii.edu
Web: http://web.hawcc.hawaii.edu/hawcc/forestteam/

Societies and Organizations

The Hawaii Forest Industry Association (HFIA) is dedicated to responsible forest management. It offers an annual woodworking exhibition, sponsors the Hawaii's Wood trademark, and serves as an advocate for Hawai'i's diverse forest industry—from tree planting and harvesting to creating and selling wood products.

Postal address:
Hawaii Forest Industry Association (HFIA)
P. O. Box 10216
Hilo Hawai'i 96721
Street address:
162 Kino'ole Street, #101
Hilo, Hawai'i 96720-2816
Tel: 808-933-9411; Fax: 808-933-9140
Email: info@hawaii-forest.org
Web: http://www.hawaii-forest.org/

Volunteers at the Hakalau Forest National Wildlife Refuge reforestation project (pictured: Cynthia Thurkins and Anya Tagawa)

The Nature Conservancy of Hawai'i preserves the plants, animals and natural communities that represent the diversity of life on Earth by protecting the lands and waters they need to survive. They have several projects directly related to protecting and restoring koa forest.

The Nature Conservancy of Hawai'i
923 Nu'uanu Avenue
Honolulu, HI 96817
Tel: 808-537-4508; Fax: 808-545-2019
E-mail: hawaii@tnc.org
Web: http://nature.org/wherewework/northamerica/states/hawaii/

The Society of American Foresters (SAF) is the national scientific and educational organization representing the forestry profession in the United States. It has an active chapter in Hawai'i. Web:
http://www.safnet.org/index.html

Tropical Reforestation & Ecosystems Education Center (TREE Center) conducts educational programs in tropical reforestation and soils conservation.

TREE Center
P.O. Box 25474
Honolulu, HI 96825-0474
Email: pam-treecenter@hawaii.rr.com
Web: http://www.treecenter.org

The Forest Stewardship Council is an international non-profit organization founded in 1993 to support environmentally appropriate, socially beneficial, and economically viable management of the world's forests.

Forest Stewardship Council, A.C.
Avenida Hidalgo 502
68000 Oaxaca, Oaxaca
Mexico
Tel: 52 951 5146905; Fax: 52 951 5162110
E-mail: fscoax@fscoax.org
Web: http://www.fscoax.org/

Hawaii Forestry and Communities Initiative supports the health and diversity of Hawai'i's native forests.
Web: http://www.state.hi.us/hfciforest/index.html

Polynesian Voyaging Society carries out voyaging programs to research and perpetuate voyaging traditions and values, develops educational programs that strengthen self-esteem and pride in history and heritage and increase caring, respect, and responsibility among individuals, families, and communities in sustaining the well-being of our special island home.

Polynesian Voyaging Society
Pier 7
191 Ala Moana Blvd.
Honolulu, HI 96813
Phone: 808-536-8405; Fax: 808-536-1519
E-mail: pvs@lava.net
Web: http://pvs-hawaii.org/

The Amy B.H. Greenwell Ethnobotanical Garden shares knowledge of Hawaiian ethnobotany, maintains a repository of native Hawaiian and Polynesian introduced plants, works for native plant conservation, and preserves an archaeological remnant of the Kona Field System on the garden site.

Amy B.H. Greenwell Ethnobotanical Garden
82-6188 Mamalahoa Highway,
Captain Cook, HI
Mailing: P.O. Box 1053,
Captain Cook, HI 96704
Tel: 808-323-3318; Fax: 808-323-2394
E-mail: pvandyke@bishopmuseum.org
Web: http://www.bishopmuseum.org/greenwell/

Rob Pacheco of Hawai'i Forest and Trail shows a snail to hikers in Kahua (Photo: Carl Waldbauer)

Trails and Hiking

Hawai'i Forest and Trail, and environmentally sensitive ecotourism company, has wonderful pages about Hawai'i's natural history, monthly nature essays, and a wealth of related links.
Web: http://www.hawaii-forest.com/

Hawai'i Volcanos National Park is a wonderful place to see native birds interacting with koa trees, particularly on the Kipuka Puaulu (Bird Park) Trail. Web: http://www.nps.gov/havo/home.htm

The Nature Conservancy of Hawai'i organizes scheduled hikes: http://nature.org/wherewework/north america/states/hawaii/

Sierra Club has regular outings: http://www.hi.sierraclub.org/

The Hawaiian Trail and Mountain Club (HTMC) is an O'ahu based hiking club founded in 1910 to explore and enjoy Hawai'i's unique natural heritage and environment.
Web: http://www.geocities.com/yosem ite/trails/3660/

Moanalua Gardens Foundation (MGF) is dedicated to preserving the native culture and environment of Hawai'i through education. Offers guided walks. Web: http://www.mgf-hawaii.com/

Na Ala Hele, Hawai'i Trail & Access System is a state program to maintain and improve the state-wide trail system has maps and descriptions of trails for all Hawaiian islands. Web: http://www.hawaiitrails.org/

Where to See Koa Trees

Hawai'i

Hawaii Volcanoes National Park
Kipuka Puaulu (Bird Park) Trail (in Volcanoes National Park)
Hakalau National Wildlife Refuge
Amy B.H. Greenwell Ethnobotanical Garden
Sadie Seymour Botanical Garden (Kona Outdoor Circle)

Maui

Haleakala National Park
Kula Botanical Garden
Makani Gardens
The Hana Road near Keanae

O'ahu

Tantalus Round Top Drive
Lyon Arboretum
Harold St. John Plant Science Laboratory courtyard
Foster Botanic Garden
Wahiawa Botanic Garden
Ho'omaluhia Botanic Garden
Waimea Arboretum and Botanical Garden
Along Likelike and Nuuanu Pali Highways

Kaua'i

The National Tropical Botanical Garden at Lawa'i
Near Kokee State Park

Web sites

Web addresses are listed throughout this chapter. As web links change rapidly (and are sometimes difficult to type), updated and clickable web links from this chapter can be found at
http://www.agroforestry.net/koa

Chapter 11: References

Abott, Isabella Aiona. 1992. Lāʻau Hawaiʻi—Traditional Hawaiian Uses of Plants. Bishop Museum Press, Honolulu.

Ares, A. and J.H. Fownes. 1999. "Water supply regulates structure, productivity, and water use efficiency of Acacia koa forest in Hawaii." In: Oecologica (1999) 121:458–466.

Ares, A., J.H. Fownes., and W. Sun. 2000. "Genetic differentiation of intrinsic water-use efficiency in the Hawaiian native Acacia koa." In: International Journal of Plant Sciences 161(6):909–915. University of Chicago.

Baker, Patrick. 2002. Personal communication. Silviculturalist, USDA Forest Service/The Nature Conservancy of Hawaii.

Bates, George W. 1854. Sandwich Island Notes, by a Haole. Harper Bros. New York.

Beaglehole, J.C. 1976. The voyage of the Resolution and Discovery, 1776–1780, Vol. 1, p. 598. Cambridge.

Beletski, L. 2000. Hawaii: The Ecotravellers' Wildlife Guide. Academic Press, London.

Bornhorst, Heidi Leianuenue. 1996. Growing Native Hawaiian Plants—A How-to Guide for the Gardener. The Bess Press, Honolulu.

Burgess, P. (Ed). 1996. From Then to Now: A Manual for Doing Things Hawaiian Style. Kaʻala Farm, Inc., P.O. Box 630, Waiʻanae, HI, 96792.

Bushe, Brian C. 2002. Personal communication. Research Associate, University of Hawaii at Manoa College of Tropical Agriculture and Human Resources Agricultural Diagnostic Service Center, Hawaii County, Hilo.

Conrad C.E., D.M. Fujii, and H. Ikawa. 1995. Seed source and performance in koa tree establishment. In: Proceedings, Hawaii Agriculture: Positioning for Growth. University of Hawaii, Honolulu.

Cuddihy, Linda W. and Charles P. Stone. 1990. Alteration of Native Hawaiian Vegetation: Effects of Humans, Their Activities, and Introductions. University of Hawaii, National Park Resources Studies Unit, Honolulu.

Culliney, J.L. 1988. Islands in a Far Sea: Nature and Man in Hawaiʻi. Sierra Club Books, San Francisco.

Dalla Rosa, Karl. 1994. Acacia koa—Hawaii's most valued native tree (NFTA 94–08). Nitrogen Fixing Tree Association, Morrilton, Arkansas.

Dawson, Ian and James Were. 1998. "Collecting germplasm from trees—some guidelines." Agroforestry Today, Vol. 9, No. 2. World Agroforestry Centre, Gigiri, Kenya.

de Jonge, Alice. 2000. Mahaweli Settlers in Sri Lanka diversify their farms using Farm Planning. In: LEISA, Dec. 2000.

Dudley, Nick. 2002. Personal communication. Research Forester, Hawaii Agriculture Research Center, Aiea.

Elevitch, Craig R. and Kim M. Wilkinson. 2000. Agroforestry Guides for Pacific Islands. Permanent Agriculture Resources, Holualoa.

Felling, Candace. 2002. Personal communication. Botanist, University of Hawaii at Manoa.

Ferentinos, L. and D.O. Evans (Eds). 1997. Koa: A Decade of Growth. Proceedings of the 1996 Annual Symposium held by the Hawaii Forest Industry Association (HFIA), November 18–19, 1996. HFIA, Hilo.

Food and Agriculture Organization (FAO) of the United Nations and NifTAL Project. 1984. Legume Inoculants and Their Use. FAO, Rome.

Friday, J.B. 2000. Acacia koa. In: CAB International, Global Forestry Compendium, CAB International, Oxford, UK.

Friday, J.B. 2002. Personal communication. Extension Forester, College of Tropical Agriculture and Human Resources, University of Hawaii at Manoa.

Fukuoka, Masanobu. 1978. The One Straw Revolution. Rodale Press, Emmaus, PA.

Gardner, D.E. 1996. Acacia koa: A review of its diseases and associated fungi. In: Koa: A Decade of Growth. Hawaii Forest Industry Association (HFIA), Hilo.

Grace K.T. 1995. Analysis and prediction of growth, grazing impacts, and economic production of Acacia koa. Ph.D. diss., Univ. of Hawaii, Honolulu.

Gustafson, R. and S.H. Sohmer. 1987. Plants and Flowers of Hawai'i. University of Hawai'i Press, Honolulu.

Habte, M. and N.W. Osorio. 2001. Arbuscular Mycorrhizas: Producing and Applying Arbuscular Mycorrhizal Inoculum. College of Tropical Agriculture and Human Resources (CTAHR), University of Hawai'i, Honolulu.

Handy, E.S. Craighill and Elizabeth G. Handy. 1972. Native Planters of Old Hawai'i: Their Life, Lore, and Environment, Bishop Museum Press, Honolulu.

Harrington R.A., J.H. Fownes, F.C. Meinzer, P.G. Scowcroft. 1995. Forest growth along a rainfall gradient in Hawaii: Acacia koa stand structure, productivity, foliar nutrients, and water- and nutrient-use efficiencies. Oecologia, 102:277–284.

Holmes, T. 1981. The Hawaiian Canoe. Editions Limited, Hanalei.

Holmgren, David. 1994. Trees on the Treeless Plains: Revegetation manual for the volcanic landscapes of Central Victoria. Holmgren Design Services, Hepburn, Australia.

Horiuchi, Baron. 2002. Personal communication. Horticulturist, Big Island National Wildlife Refuge Complex/Hakalau Forest. Hilo.

Jeffrey, Jack. 2000. Personal communication. Biologist, National Biological Service, Hilo, HI.

Jenkins, Irving. 1983. Hawaiian Furniture and Hawai'i's Cabinet Makers: 1820–1940. Daughters of Hawai'i, Honolulu.

Jones, Norman. 2001. "The Essentials of Good Planting Stock." In: The Overstory Book: Cultivating Connections with Trees. Craig R. Elevitch and Kim M. Wilkinson, Editors. Permanent Agriculture Resources (PAR), Holualoa.

Juvik, Sonia P. and James O. Juvik. Atlas of Hawai'i, Third Edition. University of Hawai'i Press, Honolulu.

Kane, Herbert Kawainui. 1997. Ancient Hawai'i. The Kawainui Press, Captain Cook.

Kepler, Angela Kay. 1984. Hawaiian Heritage Plants, The Oriental Publishing Co., Honolulu.

Keyser, Harold. Personal communication. University of Hawaii NifTAL Project, Paia.

Krauss, Beatrice H. 1993. Plants in Hawaiian Culture, University of Hawai'i Press, Honolulu.

Lamb, Samuel H. 1981. Native Trees & Shrubs of the Hawaiian Islands, Sunstone Press, Santa Fe, NM.

Landis, Tom D., R.W. Tinus, S.E. McDonald, and J.P. Barnett. 1990. The Container Tree Nursery Manual Vol. 2: Containers and Growing Media. Agricultural Handbook 674. U.S. Department of Agriculture Forest Service, Washington, DC.

Little, Elbert L. and Roger G. Skolmen. 1989. Common Forest Trees of Hawai'i (Native and Introduced). United States Department of Agriculture Forest Service, Agriculture Handbook 679.

Loudat, T.A. and R. Kanter. 1996. The Economics of Commercial Koa Culture in Hawaii. In: Koa: A Decade of Growth. Hawaii Forest Industry Association (HFIA), Hilo.

Ludvick, Jaroslav. 2002. Personal communication. Expert woodsman and harvester, retired.

MacCaughey, V. 1918. "Expedition into the Kona Forests (History of Botanical Exploration in Hawaii)." The Hawaiian Forester and Agriculturalist. Hawaiian Gazette Co., Ltd., Honolulu.

Menzies, Archibald. 1920. Hawaii Nei 128 Years Ago. Honolulu. p. 82.

Miyasaka, Susan C. 2000. Personal communication. Agronomist, Department of Tropical Plant and Soil Sciences, University of Hawaii at Manoa College of Tropical Agriculture and Human Resources, Beaumont Research Station, Hilo.

Mueller-Dombois D., and R. Fosberg. 1998. Vegetation of the Tropical Pacific Islands. Springer-Verlag, New York.

Nagata, K.M. 1992. How to Plant a Native Hawaiian Garden. State of Hawaii, Office of Environmental Quality Control, Honolulu.

Neal, Marie C. 1965. In Gardens of Hawai'i, Bishop Museum Press, Honolulu.

Pacheco, Rob. 1997. Inventory of a Koa. In: Reading the Land, Nov. 1997. web:www.hawaii-forest.com

Pang, Benton Keali'i. 1997. The Ahupua'a System and Canoe Making. In: Koa: A Decade of Growth. Hawaii Forest Industry Association (HFIA), Hilo.

Pukui, Mary Kawena, and Samuel H. Elbert. 1986. Hawaiian Dictionary (Revised and Enlarged Edition). University of Hawaii Press, Honolulu.

Pukui, Mary Kawena. 1983. Olelo No'eau: Hawaiian Proverbs and Poetical Sayings. Bishop Museum Press, Honolulu.

Rachie, Kenneth O., et al, 1979. Tropical Legumes: Resources for the Future. National Academy of Sciences, Washington, DC.

Rock, Joseph F. 1913. The Indigenous Trees of the Hawaiian Islands, 1st ed. Honolulu: Priv. published. 2nd ed. 1974. Charles E. Tuttle, Tokyo.

Scowcroft, Paul. 2000 and 2002. Personal communications. Senior Forester, USDA Forest Service Institute of Pacific Islands Forestry, Hilo.

Shigo, Alex. Tree Basics. Shigo and Trees, Associates. Durham, New Hampshire.

Simmons, Peter. 2002. Personal communication. Senior Land Manager, Kamehameha Schools, Hilo.

Skolmen, Roger G. 1986. "Where Can Koa Be Grown." In. Proceedings, Resource Conservation and Development (RC&D) Koa Conference. RC&D Forestry Committee with DLNR/DOFAW and USDA FS, Hilo.

Staples, G.W., and R.H. Cowie. 2001. Hawai'i's Invasive Species. Mutual Publishing and Bishop Museum Press, Honolulu.

Thomson, K. and F. Stubbsgaard. 1998. Easy Guide to Controlling Seed Moisture During Seed Procurement. Danida Forest Seed Centre, Humlebæk, Denmark.

Thompson, Nainoa. 2000. Hawai'iloa, 1990-1995. Polynesian Voyaging Society, Hawai'i. Web: www.pvs-hawaii.org

Wadsworth, Frank H. 1997. Forest Production for Tropical America. United States Department of Agriculture Forest Service, Agriculture Handbook 710.

Wagner W.L., D.R. Herbst, and S.H.Sohmer. 1999. Manual of the Flowering Plants of Hawaii, Revised edition. University of Hawaii Press, Honolulu.

Walker, Ron. "Koa and Wildlife—An Enduring Relationship." 1986. In: Proceedings, Resource Conservation and Development (RC&D) Koa Conference. RC&D Forestry Committee with DLNR/DOFAW and USDA FS, Hilo.

Whitcomb, Carl E. 1988. Plant Production in Containers. Lacebark Publications, OK.

Whitesell, Craig D. 1990. Acacia koa A. Gray. In: Burns, R.M., and B. Honkala. Silvics of North America Vol. 2: Hardwoods. USDA Forest Service Handbook No. 654, 17–28.

Other Titles by the Authors

The Overstory Book:

Cultivating Connections with Trees

"A concise source of pertinent information, a resource packed with practical advice and innovations."—Adam Tomasek, World Wildlife Fund, Washington, DC

"An excellent guide...which will be enjoyed and valued both by newcomers and old hands. Covers the background science, as well as detailing practical information."—The New Agriculturalist

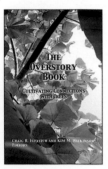

"Well-written and informative...highly recommended."—Agroforestry Systems

Whether in a small backyard or a larger farm or forest, trees are vital to the web of life. Protecting and planting trees can restore wildlife habitat, heal degraded land, conserve soil, protect watersheds, beautify landscapes, and enhance the economic and ecological viability of land use systems.

The Overstory Book distills essential information about working with trees into 72 easy-to-read, single-subject chapters. Each chapter shares key concepts and useful information, so readers can plant and protect more trees and forests, more effectively.

Available as a book or CD-ROM.

The Overstory Book: Cultivating Connections with Trees, edited by Craig R. Elevitch and Kim M. Wilkinson. 5 1/4" X 8 1/4", 430 pages, illustrated and fully indexed. ISBN 0–9702544–1–5. $39.95 for book; $16.95 for CD; $49.95 for book and CD together.

Agroforestry Guides for Pacific Islands

"Well-researched, concise, user-friendly...an invaluable practical resource."—Asia-Pacific Agroforestry News, United Nations/FAO

"A significant contribution...appropriate for use in classrooms, research stations, or privately held lands. The appealing style and format, easy readability, and helpful illustrations all contribute to this book's appeal to a wide-ranging audience."—Agroforestry Systems

"The *Guides* are rich sourcebooks for ideas and possibilities for agroforestry and include information on hundreds of useful trees and plants."—Hawai'i Forestry News

"Eloquently makes a case for reintroducing and emphasizing trees in our island agriculture."—Dr. Bill Raynor, The Nature Conservancy, Pohnpei, Micronesia

Pacific Islanders were once among the most self-sufficient and well-nourished peoples in the world. Traditional agricultural systems integrated trees with production, a practice known as agroforestry. Today, agroforestry is a vital part of sustainable farming, gardening, and conservation. *Agroforestry Guides* provide key planning information for educators, gardeners, farmers, foresters, and landscapers.

Agroforestry Guides for Pacific Islands, edited by Craig R. Elevitch and Kim M. Wilkinson. 239 pages, 8.5" X 11" soft cover binding, illustrated, fully indexed. ISBN 0–9702544–0–7. Sept 2000. $24.95.

To order these titles or additional copies of *Growing Koa*, ask at your local bookstore or order on-line from www.agroforestry.net Publisher's address: PAR, P.O. Box 428, Holualoa, HI 96725 USA; 808-324-4427; Fax: 808-324-4129; email: pubs@agroforestry.net

About the Authors

Kim M. Wilkinson

Working with tree planting people on six of the Hawaiian Islands, Kim learned about challenges koa growers face and ways they succeed. Over the past decade, Kim has grown hundreds of thousands of trees for Forest Stewardship and other reforestation projects throughout Hawai'i. She pioneered the nursery use of ecological practices such as inoculation with rhizobia and mycorrhizal fungi for koa. Kim has B.A. degrees in Anthropology and Human/Natural Ecology from Emory University, is certified in Permaculture (a 2-year ecological design program based in Australia), and is a Master Gardener.

Craig R. Elevitch

A koa grower since 1989, Craig is dedicated to research and education. He has conducted numerous research projects and seed source trials in cooperation with organizations including Cornell University, the Oxford Forestry Institute, the University of Hawai'i, and the USDA SARE Program. Craig has a Master's degree in Electrical Engineering (Dynamical Systems) from Cornell University. In his former role as a Management Planner, he worked with tree-growing projects throughout Hawai'i, including authoring a dozen Forest Stewardship Management Plans.

Kim and Craig co-direct PAR, an educational organization dedicated to empowering people in reforestation, agroforestry, and ecological resource management. The organization's internationally recognized publications have guided thousands of readers to become more proficient in ecological restoration, conservation, and reforestation, whether in a backyard, farm, or conservation area.

PAR's activities include:

- Publishing *The Overstory*, a bimonthly agroforestry journal with subscribers in over 160 countries.
- Organizing workshops and field days, with over 700 growers and resource professionals in Hawai'i participating since 1992.
- Producing educational materials, including the book *Agroforestry Guides for Pacific Islands*, a widely-acclaimed manual for integrating trees.
- Facilitating the restoration and planting of native and traditional Pacific Island trees through *The Traditional Tree Initiative*

Growing Koa is their third book.

About the Sponsors

Born and raised in Hawai'i, Muriel and Kent Lighter have a deep love of trees and the land. They are reforesting 100 acres of former pasture with koa and other trees on their farm, Kohala Nui Farms. Although the project is in an area that is difficult for growing koa, Muriel and Kent have a pioneering spirit, and are succeeding through hard work and innovations.

In the harsh, windy conditions, the Lighters are happy if about half of the koa seedlings they plant survive. Windbreaks have also been planted to protect future koa plantings from the fierce Kohala winds.

Some of their goals include genetic preservation of koa for future generations, provenance trials of seedlings from select koa seed sources, and experimenting with sustainable and organic management practices. The koa trees are being interplanted with other native and high value trees, to add to the diversity, health, and value of the planting. Experimentation is also being done with crops that can live in the understory of the forest plantings. Other areas of the project include planting native trees such as 'ōhi'a lehua and sandalwood. The plan is to have at least half the forest in koa and other native trees.

Their two children, Moses and Christina, are helping with the koa tree planting and learning how to better care for the 'aina.

Muriel and Kent Lighter's generous contribution made possible the publication of this book and supported the donation of over 250 copies of *Growing Koa* to schools, libraries, and educational organizations throughout the Hawaiian Islands.

Mahalo nui loa!

Muriel and Kent Lighter in a stand of 4-year old koa trees, part of their 100 acre reforestation project

Index